24 FOOTPAT
IN
HERTFOR

BILL FROST

PUBLISHED BY

ST ALBANS AND DISTRICT FOOTPATHS SOCIETY

(Reg. Charity 1039715)

First Edition 1992
Second Edition 1996
Third Edition 2000
Fourth Edition 2004
Fifth Edition 2010

INTRODUCTION

The St Albans & District Footpath Society was inaugurated in 1967 and this book, first published in 1992 as a companion to our other book *'**24 Footpath Walks around St Albans**'*, consists of a varied collection of favourite walks by members of the Society.

The walks, varying in length from 5.3 miles to 14.2 miles, including one of only 3.5 miles suitable for people with pushchairs or wheelchairs, are circular, using definitive or permissive paths and generally described in a clockwise direction. Counter clockwise makes an interesting variation. Frequent compass directions given in the text should prevent the walker from straying off-course when crossing open country.

All text and maps have been checked and any amendments made, but changes can occur quickly and landmarks disappear. However, details in this book are accurate at the time of going to press, but, due to circumstances out of our control, the Society cannot accept responsibility for any changes that may occur over time, nor for any accident sustained by walkers whilst using this book.

The Society would be grateful for readers' observations concerning obstructions, overgrowth or insufficient waymarking. The Countryside Access Officer at Hertfordshire County Council should be informed.

Bill Frost
2010

High Street, Wheathampstead

The Society organises walks on Thursdays and most Sundays, helps to keep footpaths clear in the St Albans District, has a programme of social events during the winter months, and publishes this book and another entitled *'**24 Footpath Walks around St Albans**'*.

Further information about the Society may be obtained by searching for 'St Albans Footpaths Society' at ***www.hertsdirect.org***

FOREWORD

COUNCILLOR CHRIS OXLEY
THE MAYOR OF THE CITY AND DISTRICT OF ST ALBANS

I commend this updated brown book to all walkers of whatever level seeking to enjoy the wonderful countryside around Hertfordshire. It complements a further 24 walks in the Society's green book *'**24 Footpath Walks around St Albans**'*.

This book gives the reader a clear and concise guide of the suggested routes. Considerable work has gone into ensuring the explanations are clear and accurate, so that you can use the book with confidence.

Please support the refreshment establishments where they are indicated, as they provide that extra bonus to what I hope you will find are magnificent walks. Sadly if we do not use them, they will not continue to be available over the coming years, which I believe will be a great loss to the character of local communities.

Mayor and President 2009/2010

ACKNOWLEDGEMENTS

Many members of St Albans Footpaths Society have been involved with the publication and updating of this book since it was first issued in 1992, when it was proposed by the late Gordon Rowe. Bill Frost has played a major role with each edition, preparing maps and editing text.

In later editions, Peter Lawrence and many members of the society have checked paths and updated scripts and maps. Mavis Wyn-Ruffhead designed the outer cover and was responsible for many of the illustrations. Some drawings by John Howes are now included.

Jane Kerr has now brought this edition to print and also organises distribution.

We thank everyone for their contribution.

MAPS

The Ordnance Survey Maps relevant to the walks in this book are :

LANDRANGER scale 1:50000
Aylesbury and Leighton Buzzard No. 165
Luton, Hertford and surrounding area No. 166

EXPLORER scale 1:25000
Chiltern Hills North No. 181
St Albans, Hatfield, Hemel Hempstead and Welwyn Garden City No. 182
Luton, Stevenage, Hitchin and Ampthill No. 193
Hertford, Bishops Stortford, Buntingford and Clavering No. 194

DEFINITIVE scale 1:10000. These show all the Rights of Way in Hertfordshire and information as to where these can be seen can be found at ***www.hertsdirect.org/row***. Reference to these should be made whenever there is doubt about a route or the status of any particular path.

GRID REFERENCES FOR PARKING

Parking for each walk is found by its Grid Reference. To locate these, read the first three numbers of the reference along the top or bottom edges of the Ordnance Survey map, i.e. in an easterly direction from L to R. So numbers 147 mean that from line 14 go 7 small divisions towards line 15 to get a vertical direction. Then read the last three numbers along the vertical edges, i.e. in a northerly direction to get a horizontal direction. The intersection of these two directions gives the map location for parking.

In this example,
G.R. 147,268 locates
the Church.
The road junction is at
G.R. 142,263

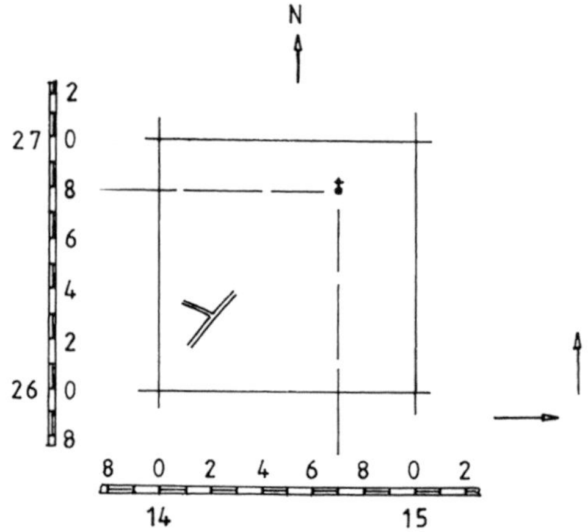

RIGHTS OF WAY ACT 1990

This Act states that :

(a) Paths around the edge of a field must not be ploughed or disturbed.
(b) Paths across a field may be ploughed and cropped but must be restored within 14 days.
(c) Restoration means making good the surface to make it useable by walkers. Moreover, the line of the path must be apparent on the ground so that walkers can see where it goes through crops.
(d) The minimum path width must be 1 metre for a footpath across fields and 1.5 metres for a footpath around a field edge.

If readers experience any problems concerning paths mentioned in this book, please notify the Countryside Access Officer of Hertfordshire County Council or the Secretary of the Ramblers Association (see below). Quote the date, the Walks Booklet reference and the location given by a six figure Grid Reference or a copy of the O.S. map to highlight the problem.

Ramblers Association :
2nd Floor, Camelford House, 87-90 Albert Embankment, London SE1 7TW
Tel : 020 7339 8500 Fax : 020 7339 8501 Email : ramblers@ramblers.org.uk

REMEMBER THE COUNTRY CODE

Be safe, plan ahead and follow any signs
Leave gates and property as you find them
Protect plants and animals and take your litter home
Keep dogs under close control
Consider other people

This is the most recent version of the Code issued in 2004. More information on the five points listed above is available on-line at :

www.countrysideaccess.gov.uk

Organisations can obtain multiple copies of the Code by telephoning 0870 120 1273.

LEGEND

Symbol	Description
═══════	Motorway
═══════	Main Road
───────	Secondary Road
= = = = =	Track or Lane
───▬───	Railway
─ ▫ ─ ▫ ─	Overhead Power Line (OHP)
─ ─ ─ ─ ─	Path
═══─ ─ ─	Fenced Path
†	Church
×	Signpost
^	Waymark. Yellow for footpaths, Blue for bridleways, Red for byways
⊢⊣	Stile
G	Gate / Kissing Gate
f. b.	Footbridge
PH	Public House
🌳🌳🌳	Woodland Trees
L , R	The walkers left or right when walking the specified route
(N) (S) (E) (W)	Compass points
m	Metres
G. R.	Grid References
C. P.	Car Park
Wr Twr	Water Tower

CONTENTS

WALK 1

Great Offley Church

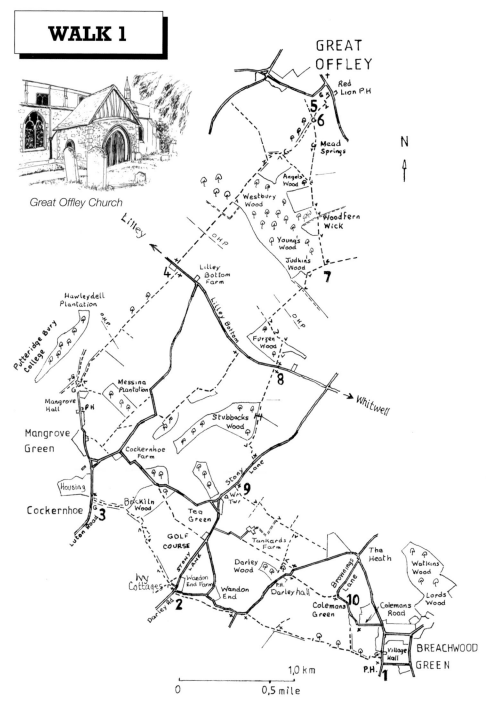

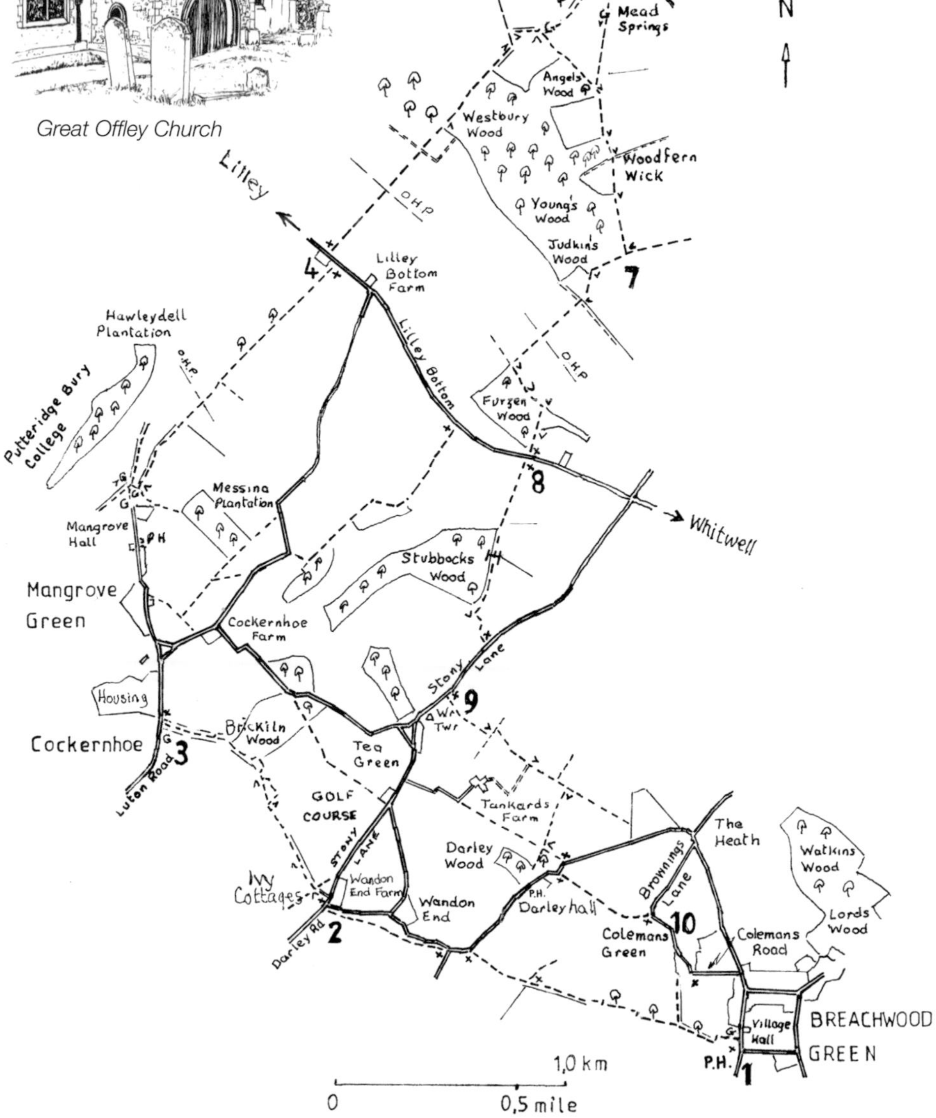
GREAT OFFLEY
Red Lion P.H
5
6
Mead Springs
N
Angels Wood
Westbury Wood
Woodfern Wick
Young's Wood
Judkins Wood
7
Lilley
OHP
Lilley Bottom Farm
4
Hawleydell Plantation
Putteridge Bury College
Lilley Bottom
Furzen Wood
OHP
8
Whitwell
Messina Plantation
Mangrove Hall
P.H
Mangrove Green
Stubbocks Wood
Cockernhoe Farm
Housing
Stony Lane
9
Wr Twr
Brickiln Wood
Cockernhoe
3
Luton Road
Tea Green
GOLF COURSE
Tankards Farm
Stony Lane
Darley Wood
The Heath
Watkins Wood
Ivy Cottages
Wandon End Farm
Wandon End
P.H.
Darley hall
Brownings Lane
10
Colemans Green
Colemans Road
Lords Wood
Darley Rd
2
Village Hall
BREACHWOOD GREEN
P.H.
1
1,0 km
0
0,5 mile

Total Distance 8.7 miles (14 km)

BREACHWOOD GREEN, COCKERNHOE, MANGROVE GREEN, OFFLEY

WALK 1

Park in public car park at the village hall, Breachwood Green. G.R.151,219

WALK 1:

As the Village Hall CP is no longer available for public use, park considerately in Chapel Road, Breachwood Green. GR.151-219.

The text at ***Alternatively*** should be numbered 5, with following Paragraphs ***re-numbered*** 6 to 10 to align with the map.

1 From the car park, turn L (S) along the road and in 100m cross the road to the signposted kissing ... Take this path (W) past some trees L and through a zig-zag turn. Continue (W) and ... at a right-angle bend and immediately L, continuing (W) on a grassy path. ... R and in 30m turn L, to follow a signposted bridleway (W), eventually ...oad. Turn L (W) along this road for 100m to the next road junction L. ...rallel to Darley Road R, which follows this road (W) to a T-junction with ... at Wandon End Farm R, continue (W) and cross a grassy island to the ...

2 ...ack passing Ivy Cottages L to reach a path marked 'Cockernhoe Green'. ... Soon a diversion around a small tree plantation is waymarked, but then ...y of Brickkiln Wood the path bears L (NW). At the far side is another small tree plantatio... ...ked diversion. Continue (W) between fence and hedge out to Luton Road at Cockernhoe.

3 Turn R (N) along this road to Mangrove Green. Go through the village (N). Ignoring path R, continue past the King William PH. Go through a gate to the brick wall boundary of Putteridge Bury College, turn sharp R (SE) away from this wall and in 30m turn L (NE) along a farm track with hedge L. This clear path, marked by some trees, continues (NE) for 1.3km to a signpost in Lilley Bottom Road.

4 Cross the road, turn L and in 40m turn R (NE) at a signpost, to a path across fields. Go down hill, then up towards Westbury Wood. Continue (NE) along the wood boundary R. On leaving the wood the path soon turns (N) with hedge R. In 50m at a path junction, turn R (E) with hedge L. In a further 80m where the path turns R, bear L (NE) through a gate, follow a hedge L (NE) for 400m to a gate at the lower corner of the field.

Alternatively : If you require refreshments or wish to visit Great Offley, go through the gate and continue (NE) round the pumping station and out to the road opposite The Red Lion PH. Return through this gate to continue the walk.

5 To resume the return journey, walk (S) to a waymarked stile, cross and continue diagonally across the field to the corner of Angel's Wood. Continue (S) across a field to the boundary of another wood at Woodfern Wick. Cross a track and continue alongside the edge of Young's Wood R to a crossing track at Judkin's Wood.

6 Here turn R (SW) alongside the wood edge for 200m. At the next corner of the wood bear L (S). In about 100m go through the hedge gap and continue (SW) downhill. In a further 400m reach the corner of Furzen Wood. Turn L (SE) around the wood and follow the path into the wood edge. In 200m look for a waymark R at low level. Here bear R (S) through the wood and zig-zag through trees to emerge and follow the wood boundary R. Continue (S) down to Lilley Bottom Road.

7 Cross the road to a clear path opposite, which goes uphill (S) along the boundary of Stubbocks Wood R. Here are good views of the surrounding countryside. Continue ahead over a stile along the edge of the wood with fence R. The path soon zig-zags downhill (S) then (SE) to a signpost in Stony Lane. Turn R along this lane (SW) towards the water tower at Tea Green. In 300m just before the first cottage L, turn L (SE) at a signpost.

8 Look for a path between fields with oak trees 20m on R. This continues (SE) past the end of an access track from Tankards Farm. Ignoring this track, continue for 200m (SE) to a path junction where turn R (SW) towards Darley Wood. Before reaching the wood boundary, turn L (SE) alongside the wood R and out to Darley Road at a signpost. Turn R and in 20m where the road bends R, turn L on a signposted path (SE). This emerges onto a road at Brownings Cottage.

9 Turn R (SE) along Brownings Lane for 300m. Where this lane turns L at Colemans Farm, bear R through a gap. Keep L (S) and in 200m meet the tree-lined outward path in Item 1. Turn L (E), along a short L and R out to the road and so to the car park in Breachwood Green.

WALK 2

Ley Green

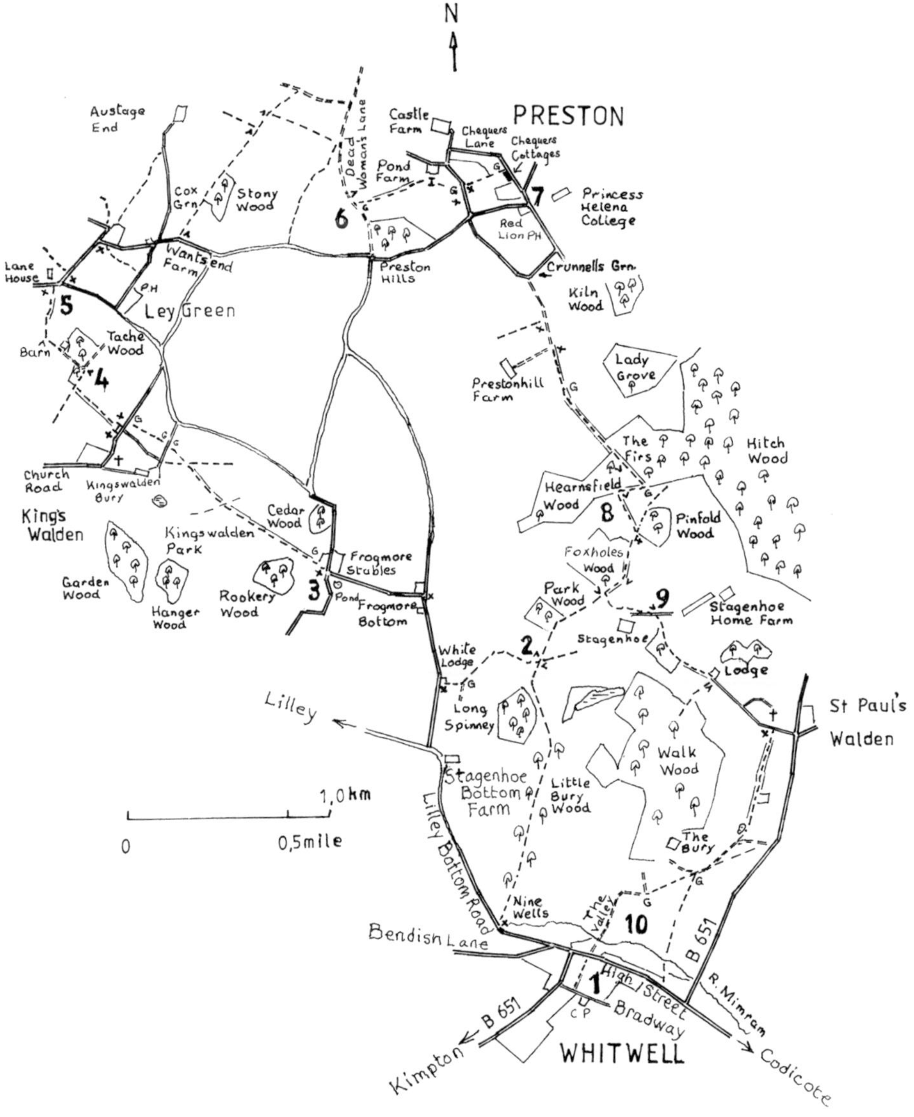

Total Distance 9.1 miles (14.6 km)

WHITWELL, KING'S WALDEN, PRESTON, ST PAUL'S WALDEN

WALK 2

Park in Whitwell recreation ground car park in Bradway. G.R.183,210

1 From the car park, turn L and immediately R (N) down Oldfield Rise. Continue along the housing path into Buttons Lane and out to the High Street. Turn L (W) along Lilley Bottom Road towards Lilley, passing the watercress beds and River Mimram R. At the end of the beds turn R (N) into a signposted track. Continue for 1.25km over the hill down to a crossing track with Long Spinney L.

2 Turn L (W) on a wide track, which bends (SW). Ignoring the farm track L, turn R (W) along a grass path towards the white house and out to a road. Turn R (N) along this road and in 400m at Frogmore Bottom, turn L (W) to a T-junction with a pond L at Frogmore Stables R.

3 At the lodge and signpost opposite, go through a gate into Kingswalden Park. Continue (NW) following waymarks, cross a farm track to a gate at a driveway. Go through the gate opposite and continue (NW) across a field passing Kingswalden Bury L to the corner gate into Church Road. Here turn L (SW) and in 40m turn R (NW) at a signpost. Follow this path with hedge L to Tache Wood, where turn R along the boundary of the wood.

4 In 70m this meets a farm track at a bend. Turn L along this track (NW), with hedge R, go past a barn R. Bear R (N) around a field edge, follow the hedge R to a hedge gap at the road, opposite 'Lane House' in Ley Green.

5 Cross the road, turn R and immediately L at the signpost 'Preston Hitchin' (NE). This road shortly turns R at a similar signpost. Go downhill past Wantsend Farm L and pond R. Continue ahead up the road (E) and in 70m turn L (NE) at a by-way sign. (This path has bluebells in season). Ignore path junctions L and R. At a T-junction the track bears R (E) to another T-junction with a grassy track, known as Dead Woman's Lane. Turn R (S) along it and in 500m at a signposted gate turn L (E).

6 Cross the field to a waymarked stile, continue along the track to a barn, where bear R (SE) away from Pond Farm L, then down a slope towards housing. Go through a hidden gate into the lane. Turn L (N) and in 20m turn R (E) at a signpost on a path alongside housing R into Chequers Lane. Turn R (SE), passing Chequers Cottages R, to a junction with the main road. Continue ahead (SE) to Preston village green with The Red Lion PH opposite.

7 Continue along this road (SE) with brick wall of Princess Helena College L. In about 250m opposite the main gate, turn R (SW) along Crunnells Green road. In 200m where this road bends R, turn L (S) at the signpost along a metalled access road. Where this turns R to Prestonhill Farm, continue ahead along the signposted grass path (S). Continue (SE) between a fence L and hedge R into woodland called The Firs. At the far boundary, turn sharp R (W) to follow the edge of the wood R.

8 In 100m go through the gap in the hedge, turn L (SE) to follow this hedge L towards a cottage. Turn R (SW) just past this cottage. Follow the boundary of Foxholes Wood R, on a path which enters the wood alongside its boundary (SW) for the last 100m. On emerging from the wood, at a field corner R, turn L (SE) at the waymark towards the driveway to Stagenhoe. Follow the path parallel to this driveway R (E) then cross it.

9 Continue (SE) round the tennis court R along a track with woods R to a red brick wall L. This track continues into a road (SE) to St Paul's Walden Church L. At the signpost opposite the church gate, turn R (S) down a track past the walled garden L, bear R onto a driveway. In 250m where this bends R, continue ahead through a kissing gate into a field. Here two paths meet. Take the fork R (W) diagonally across the field to another gate into a gravel track.

10 In 100m this track bends L (S) downhill to cross the River Mimram into housing. This becomes a road called The Valley and meets the High Street, opposite Buttons Lane. Continue up Buttons Lane into Oldfield Rise, turning L at Bradway to return to the car park.

WALK 3

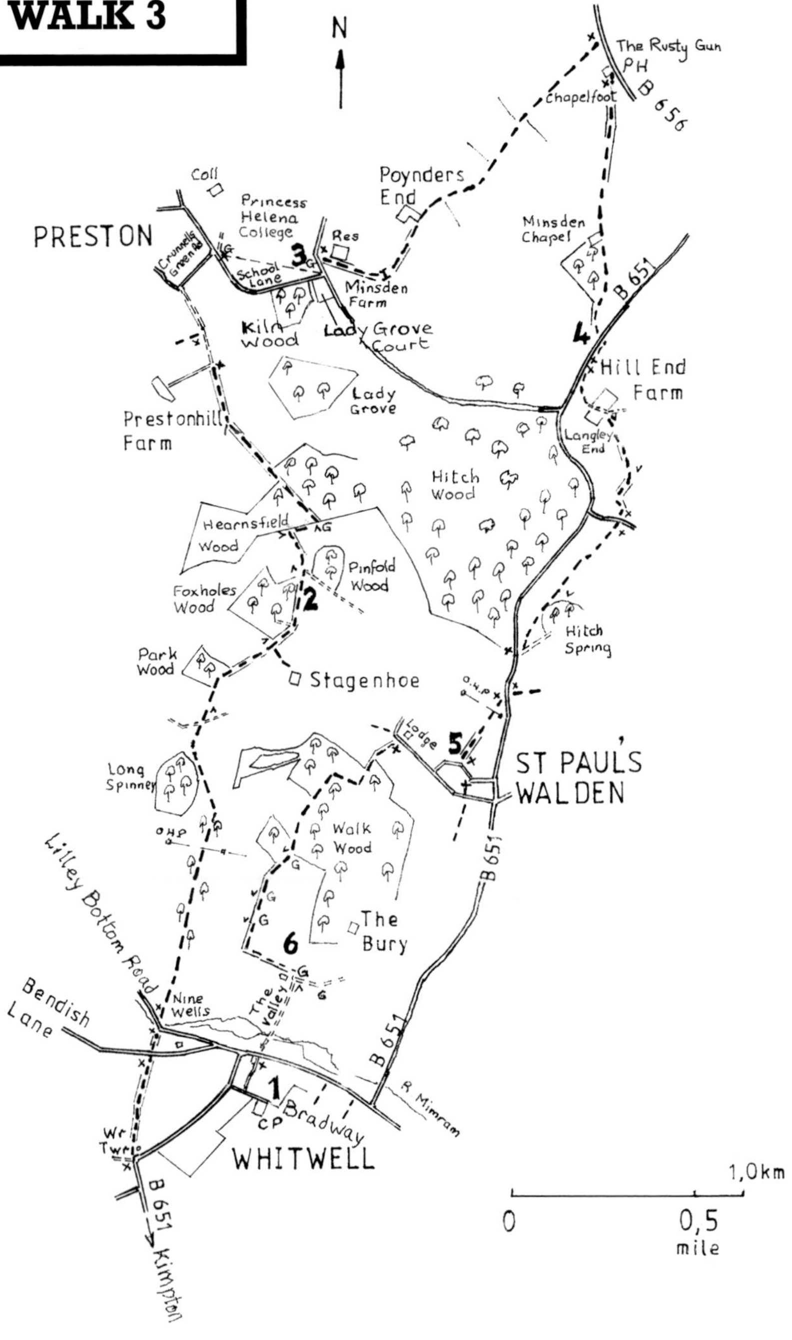

Total Distance 8.3 miles (13.4 km)

WHITWELL, CHAPELFOOT, ST PAUL'S WALDEN

WALK 3

Park in Whitwell recreation ground car park in Bradway. G.R.183,210

1 From the car park, turn L along Bradway to Kimpton Road (B651). Turn L (SW) uphill to the water tower. Turn R round the tower into the signposted by-way (N) down to Bendish Lane. Cross and continue down to Lilley Bottom Road at the watercress beds. Turn L and in 5m (N) pass 'Nine Wells' R into a tree-lined track. After about 1.25km, go over a crossing track, continue (N) at a waymark along the edge of Park Wood. Continue (NE) with hedge R and fence L along the edge of Foxholes Wood. On emerging at the corner of the wood, bear L (N), and follow the edge of the wood L to a red brick house.

2 Go round the house, turn L (NW) along the access track. In 50m bear R and follow a hedge R to Hearnsfield Wood. Turn R (E) along the boundary of this wood L, and in 150m turn L (NW) at the waymarked gate into the wood itself. Continue (N) with fence R then between hedges to meet an access road near Prestonhill Farm. Continue (N) along this to the T-junction then turn R (NE) along Crunnells Green. At the junction with School Lane, cross road and pass through a kissing gate to the R of entrance to Princess Helena College and follow permissive path (E) across field, signposted 'Lady Grove', to road junction at Minsden Farm.

3 Turn L (NW) and in 60m turn R (SE) along a fenced path with a reservoir L. Continue (NE) around the edge of a field with hedge R, then over a stile and with hedge L to Poynders End Farm. Continue (NE) downhill to the Hitchin road (B656). Turn R (S) to The Rusty Gun PH. Just beyond this, bear R (S) at the signposted, fenced track uphill. Note the ruins of Minsden Chapel R at the corner of a small wood, continue (S) down to the B651.

4 Cross the road to a signposted path opposite. This goes uphill (S) to meet the access road leading to Langley End. Turn L (SE), go past 'Bridle Ways' L, then when this road turns L, continue ahead (S) at the waymark. Continue through gaps with hedge R, then between hedges to the road. Cross the road to a path opposite, cross a field to a gap by a small wood at the top of the hill. Continue (SW) to a track which leads to the B651. Turn L (S), pass the entrance to the Sue Ryder Home, Stagenhoe R and in about 200m turn R to a path at a signpost. Bear L under the power lines (SW) and follow a line of trees to fenced path between houses to a narrow road.

5 Turn R (NW) to a T-junction. Turn R again (NW) for 200m to a red brick wall R. Opposite this turn L (SW) along a path between hedges. Follow this path as it winds through the wood, then along its edge L to a gate into an open field with wood R. Continue downhill with hedge R to a corner where the path turns L (SE) with the fence R to a gate R. Go through, turn L to a bend in a lane.

6 Turn R (S) downhill towards the village on a track called The Valley, which crosses the river and emerges onto the High Street, opposite Buttons Lane. Continue up Buttons Lane into Oldfield Rise, turning L on reaching Bradway to return to the car park.

WALK 4

The Valley, Whitwell

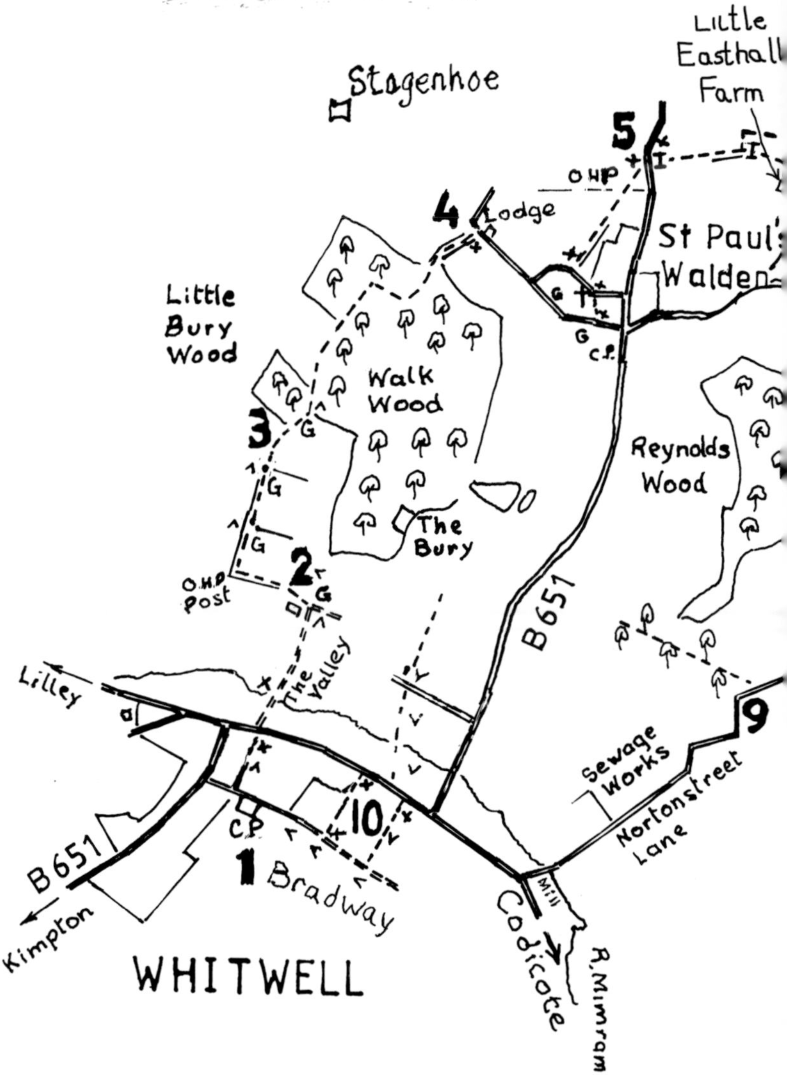

Total Distance 6.4 miles (10.3 km)

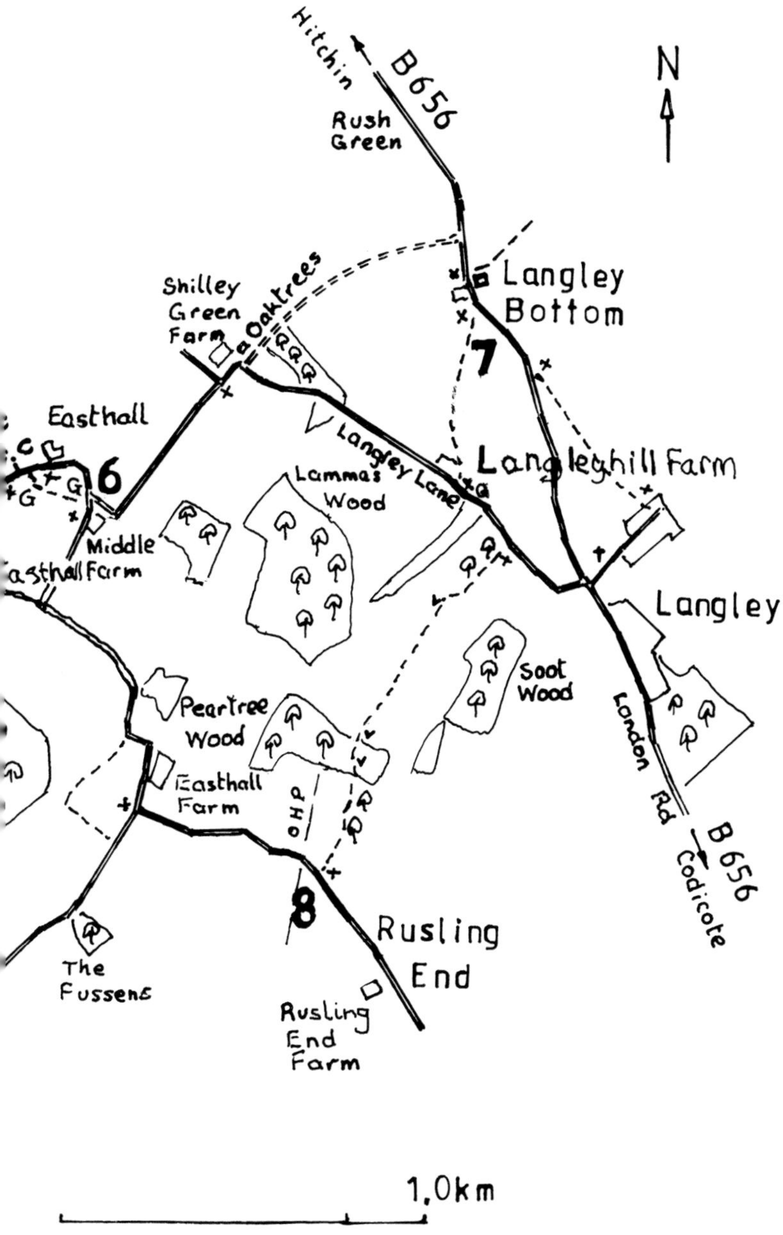
Hitchin
B656
Rush Green
N
Langley Bottom
Shilley Green Farm
Oaktrees
7
Easthall
6
Langley Lane
Langleyhill Farm
Lammas Wood
Middle Easthall Farm
Langley
Soot Wood
Peartree Wood
London Rd
Easthall Farm
OHP
B656
Codicote
8
Rusling End
The Fussens
Rusling End Farm
1,0km
0
0,5mile

WHITWELL, EASTHALL, LANGLEY

WALK 4

Park in Whitwell recreation ground car park in Bradway.
G.R.183,210

1 From the car park, turn L and immediately R (N) down Oldfield Rise. Continue along housing path into Buttons Lane out to the High Street. Cross the road into the road opposite called The Valley, noting the fine timbered house R. Follow this road (N) over the River Mimram onto a track uphill for 250m to a T-junction.

2 Turn L (W) and immediately in front of the iron gate, turn R into a field. Turn L (W) to follow the hedge L to a power line post at the corner of this field. Turn R (N) following another hedge L, climb along the field edge and go through a swing gate into another field. (Note the woodlands of The Bury R, childhood home of the HM Queen Elizabeth, the late Queen Mother).

3 Continue (N) with hedge then a wood L, go through a swing gate into a third field, then go through another swing gate into Little Bury Wood. A clear path continues (N) alongside the boundary of this wood L. After a short R and L diversion, the path emerges from the wood and continues between hedges (NE), with views of St Paul's Walden Church R and Stagenhoe L, to a crossing road.

4 Turn R (E), ignore a turning L, and continue to St Paul's Walden Church (where HM Queen Elizabeth, the late Queen Mother was christened). Turn L (N) through the church gate opposite the car park. Go past the church L into a minor road, where turn L (NW). In 80m turn R (NE) onto a narrow signposted path between garden fences. Continue (NE) along a field path, with fence and hedge R. Pass a power line junction to a road at a signpost and hedge gap near a large oak.

5 Cross this road with care and the stile opposite. Cross the field (E) past a large oak tree and water trough R. Continue (E) with hedge R to a stile in the hedge corner. Do not cross this stile, but turn L along permissive path and in 20m at corner turn R, passing row of trees R and go through gate. Cross small field and go through next gate to minor road. Turn L (NE) and almost immediately, opposite a cottage with steep gables, turn R through a gate (SE) into a field with hedge R. Continue past large field gates R to a signpost and gate at road junction L.

6 Turn L and immediately R (SE) into a narrow road signposted 'Langley'. Follow this round a sharp bend L, continue (NE) past Shilley Green Farm L. At the sharp bend in the road R, continue ahead (NE) on a gravel track past 'Oaktrees' L. Follow downhill past a wood R to its junction with the B656, the Hitchin to Welwyn road. Turn R along the grass verge for 250m through Langley Bottom to a signposted bridleway, where turn R (S).

7 Follow this bridleway uphill with hedge R into Langleyhill Farm. Go through the farmyard with farmhouse R to a road. Turn L (SE) along this, past a small wood R and in 200m look for a bridleway R with row of trees R. This bridleway climbs gently, then continues (SW) downhill across a field to enter a wood as a wide track. Follow this track (S) through the wood to emerge with hedge L onto a minor road at a signpost.

8 Turn R along this road (NW) for 600m. At the T-junction by corner cottages R, turn L (SW) onto a broad track between hedges, this is known as Nortonstreet Lane. In 700m, after a wooded area L, note a short track R where in a few metres there is a distant view (NW) of The Bury at the end of an avenue of limes.

9 Continue (SW) downhill, past the sewage works R. Keep straight on, crossing the River Mimram to Codicote Road. Turn R (NW) past cottages with raised gardens L to house No.22 in the High Street. This enables you to see more of the village.

10 Opposite No.22, turn L (SW) at the signpost marked 'Kimpton', go uphill on a path between housing, with conifer hedge L. On emerging into a field, turn R and follow field edge R (NW), passing bungalows R. Go between tall shrubs, past tennis courts L into the car park.

St. Paul's Walden Church

WALK 5

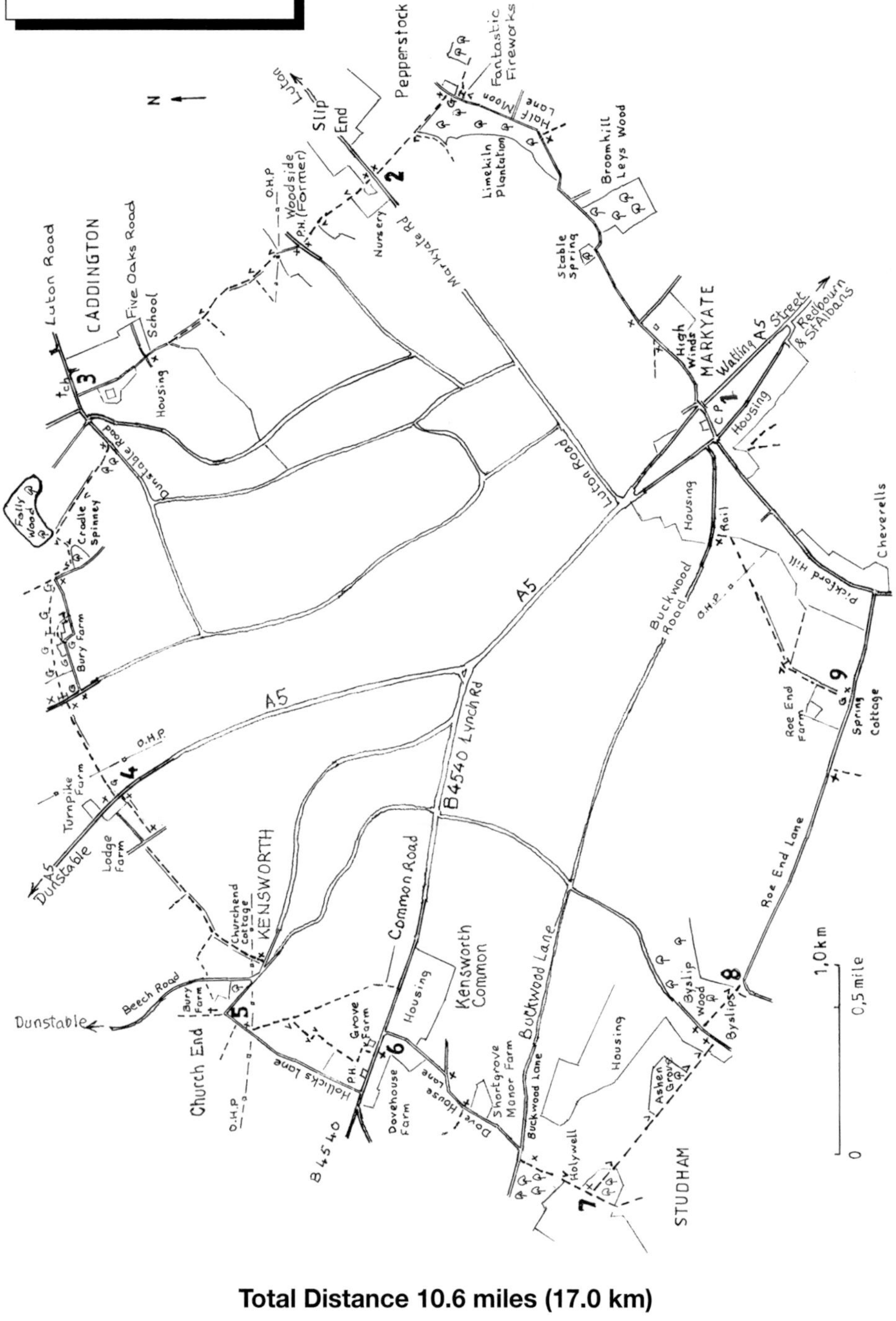

Total Distance 10.6 miles (17.0 km)

MARKYATE, SLIP END, WOODSIDE, CADDINGTON, KENSWORTH

WALK 5

Park in public car park in Hicks Road, Markyate. G.R.063,164

1 Turn L (NE) out of the car park towards the A5 and cross using the footbridge. Walk up Hicks Hill passing 'High Winds' R. Where this lane turns R, continue ahead (NE) along a track called Half Moon Lane. In about 2km at the end of the wood L opposite a gated house, turn L (NW) along a path to Markyate Road at Slip End.

2 Cross the road and continue along a path (NW) to a former PH at Woodside. Directly opposite continue along a lane past housing L. Go under power lines, across a field, then along a field edge path with hedge L. Go across a field to the school fence, bear L for 50m then R into Heathfield Path. Cross Five Oaks Road and continue (NW) through housing, passing school L, to the junction with Luton Road, opposite the church.

3 Turn L along Luton Road to a junction where Luton Road becomes Dunstable Road. Continue straight on (SW) along Dunstable Road for about 250m. Turn R (NW) opposite No.33 along a path through bushes, then with hedge R. Continue (NW) to the corner of Folly Wood, then follow the waymarks. Turn L (SW) to the corner of Cradle Spinney, then (W) alongside its boundary to the field corner. Turn R (NW) with hedge L, at a waymarked post bear L through a gap into a sunken lane. Continue along it to the buildings of Bury Farm. Here turn R alongside buildings L to a way-marked gate. Go through gate and keep R along farm road through gates to the main road. At the road turn R (NW) and in 100m turn L (SW) at the gap. This path, with hedge L, goes under power lines down to the A5, opposite Lodge Farm.

4 Turn L along A5 and in 50m R (SW) alongside a green boundary fence L by a builders yard. Continue up a field edge with hedge R to a metal gate leading to a lane. Turn R (NW) along this and in 50m turn L up a path with hedge R. This leads over a hill. Crossing to either side of hedge at two waymarks, ignore a path R and continue (SW) down to a road along which turn R (NW) to the church at Church End.

5 Turn L (SW) up Hollicks Lane. In 150m turn L (S) into a field path immediately under power lines. Cross this field (S) down to a large tree. Bear R (SW) at the waymark and continue down to the bottom of the valley, just to R of two waymarked trees. Turn L in front of them, then R (SW) following the field edge up to houses on the skyline. Turn L (SE) behind the houses for 50m then turn R through a squeeze gap onto a path between houses, then L onto a tarmac road to Common Road. If you are seeking refreshments, turn R (NW) along this road and in 100m is The Farmers Boy PH. To continue return to the housing.

6 Continue along the road (SE) and in 150m turn R into Dovehouse Lane. Pass Shortgrove Manor Farm L go on to its junction with Buckwood Lane. Turn R (W) and in 50m L (SW), go through a gap, bear R to a waymark post, then turn sharp L to follow path which veers R and up through woodland with housing R.

7 Continue with field L and housing R and after 400m turn L (SE) at the signpost through the woods, then across a field and alongside Ashen Grove L. This passes housing R and emerges onto the road at Byslips. Turn L (NE) and in 100m R (SE) along a path with woods L.

8 On emerging from the wood, turn R then L at the waymark, this joins Roe End Lane in 50m. Continue (SE) for 1.5km along this lane, joining surfaced road, past Roe End Farm.

9 In 100m past farm entrance opposite 'Spring Cottage', turn L (NE), go through the signposted gate and follow the fence R. Go through a gap and continue (NE) diagonally across the field under power lines. Turn L onto a crossing path, with housing R, to Buckwood Lane. Turn R along the road to the junction, where a short R and L leads to the car park.

WALK 6

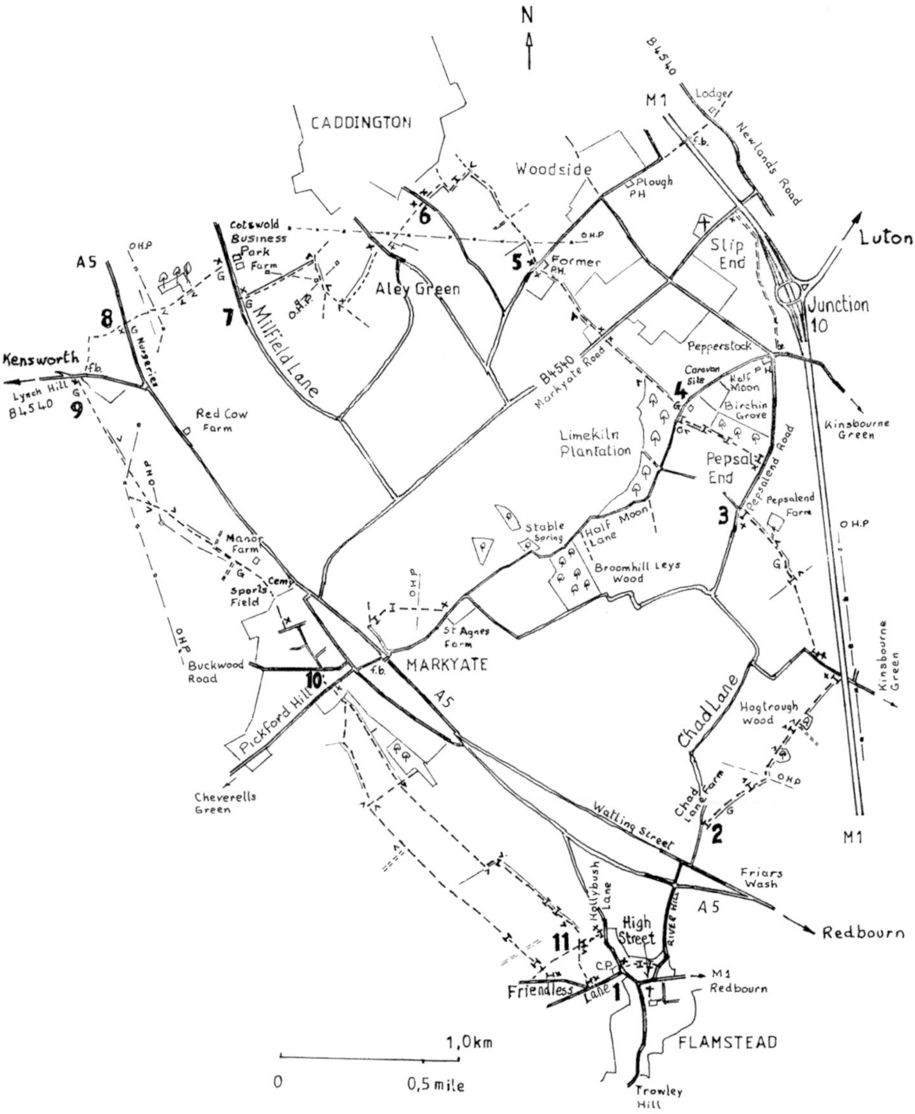

Total Distance 9.3 miles (15.0 km)
Shorter Route 6.3 miles (10.1 km)

FLAMSTEAD, PEPSAL END, MARKYATE

WALK 6

Park in Flamstead recreation ground car park at the junction of Friendless Lane and Hollybush Lane. G.R.077,147

1 From the car park, bear R (SE) along Chapel Road, then turn L (E) into High Street, in 100m turn L (N) down River Hill to the A5. Cross the road, go up the hill (N), and in 100m turn R (E) along the ancient Watling Street, then in 10m turn L (N) into Chad Lane.

2 Continue along this lane for 300m to a signpost R, opposite Chad Lane Farm. Cross the stile (NE), go along a path with hedge R and continue down into a valley, then up alongside Hogtrough Wood R into a road by the motorway. Turn L (NW) away from the M1 and in 150m at the signpost, turn R (N) across the field towards a stile in the fence. Cross and continue (NW) with fence R past Pepsalend Farm R into Pepsal End Road.

3 Turn R (NE) along this road for 300m. At the signpost turn L over a stile, and continue under power lines alongside a wood R. Cross two more stiles and go between fences into Half Moon Lane. Turn R (NE) to 'Keepers Cottage' at Birchin Grove Farm and turn L through a gate immediately opposite the cottage.

4 Continue (NW) alongside a wood boundary L, then with hedge R. Go through the hedge gap and emerge onto Markyate Road. Cross and continue forward (NW) between housing, then with hedge R, emerge by a former PH.

5 Cross the road, continue (NW) into the asphalt access track, which soon becomes a gravel track under power lines. Go forward across a field, ignore the path L at the hedge corner. Continue with hedge L to a corner where turn L (SW). In the next corner cross the iron stile, not easily seen, go ahead (SW) into the sports field. Keep to the hedge L and follow it round a R and L corner. Continue (SW) past the tennis courts R and emerge into a road at a pipe-rail gap.

6 Cross the road and continue ahead (SW) across a field under two power lines, then with hedge L emerge into the road in the valley bottom. Turn R (NW) and in 25m turn L (SW) over a plank bridge. Go uphill with hedge R to a crossing path with three-way signpost. Turn R (NW) and go forward. At the hedge gap, follow the waymark. After going under the power lines, turn L (SW) at the next hedge. Follow this R out to Millfield Lane through a gap at a double gate.

7 Turn R (N) to the Cotswold Business Park R. Opposite the entrance turn L (SW) through a signed gap by a gate. Cross the field (SW) heading for the L end of a line of trees. Continue through the wood R. On emerging from the wood, bear L across the field towards the tallest tree in the hedge, heading for the A5 road sign. Just under the power line, go through gate in the hedge by this tree. At the bottom of the next field, go through gate onto the A5 by Kensworth Nurseries.

8 Cross this busy road with care, and enter the field opposite. Go uphill for 200m (SW). At the crossing path, turn L (S) and continue down to a hedge gap by a large chestnut tree. Cross the plank bridge into Lynch Hill (B4540). Turn R (W) and in 20m turn L (SE) by a gate into a wide gravel track.

9 Go ahead (SE) into a field with hedge L, then under power lines. At a waymark by a power post, bear L through this hedge. Cross the field (SE) following the power lines R. This leads to a track with hedge L. Follow this track (SE). Where this track turns R by a power pole, keep forward (SE) by a gate gap. Go through the next gate into a sports area, follow a hedge L into a road. Turn L (NE) and in 60m turn R (SE) by a seat to a track leading to roads between housing. Cross Buckwood Road to a path alongside Markyate Baptist Church.

10 Continue ahead (SE) through housing, over a grassy area, bear L into Pickford Hill. Cross to a sunken footpath (SE) between houses Nos.19 and 21 Markyate Park. Take the L fork with hedge L (SE). Ignore first crossing path, and after a further 0.5km at a crossing hedge turn L (NE) at the waymark. In 50m just before a hedge corner, turn R (SE) over a waymarked stile. Continue (SE) with hedge L, cross three stiles to a wooden signpost, then go (S) between fences.

11 In 250m at the next wooden signpost just before the path turns R, turn L (NE), cross the stile and go over the field into Hollybush Lane. Here turn R (S) and in 150m turn R into car park.

Alternatively : This walk may be shortened by turning L at Item 4 and going down Half Moon Lane to Markyate. The route then being Items 1, 2, 3, 4, 10 and 11.

WALK 7

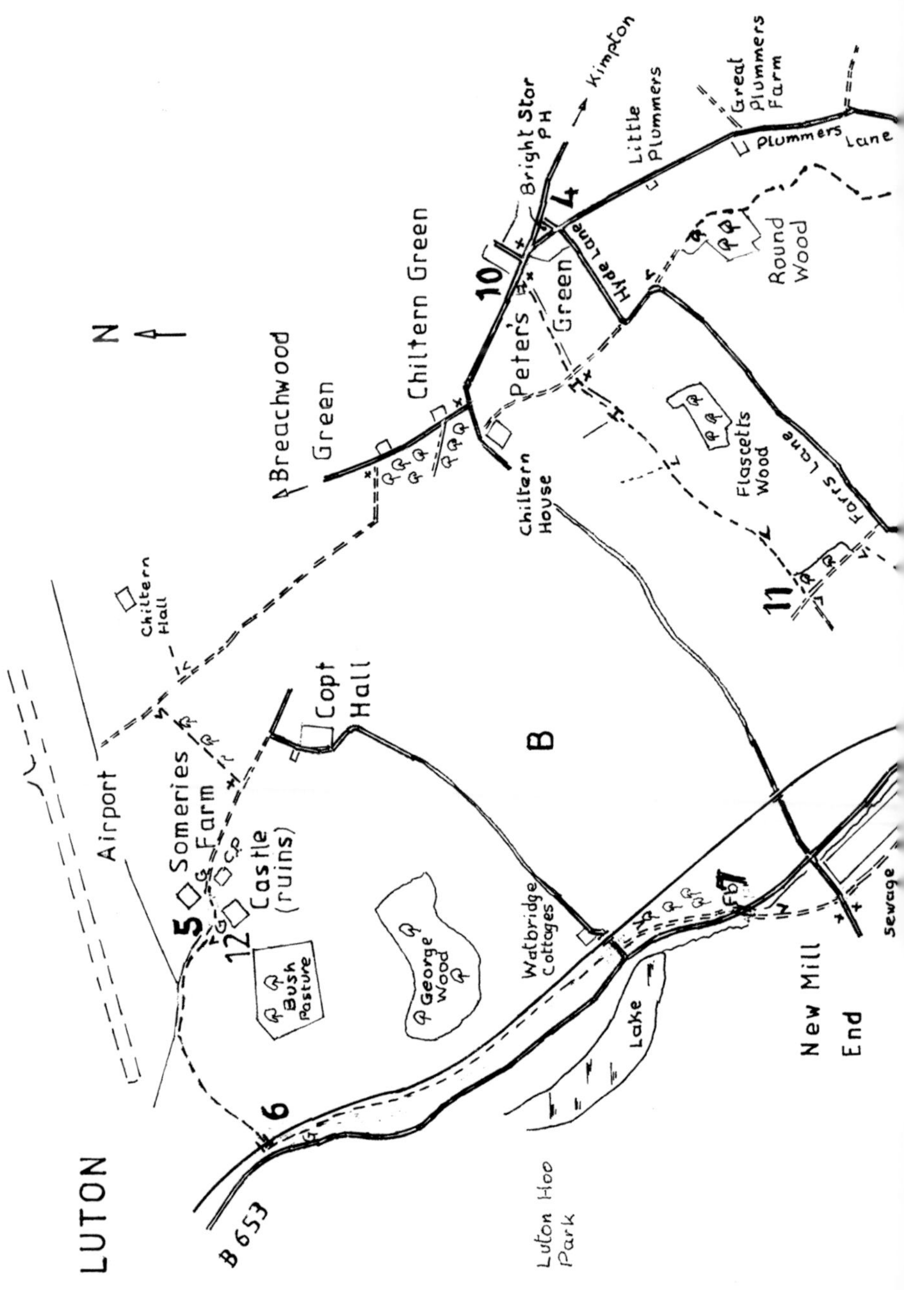
N
Breachwood Green
Chiltern Green
Kimpton
Bright Star P H
Little Plummers
Great Plummers Farm
Plummers Lane
Hyde Lane
Round Wood
Peter's Green
Flascetts Wood
Farrs Lane
Chiltern House
Chiltern Hall
Copt Hall
B
Airport
Someries Farm
Castle (ruins)
Bush Pasture
George Wood
Watbridge Cottages
Lake
New Mill End
Sewage
LUTON
B 653
Luton Hoo Park
1
2
4
5
6
10
11
12

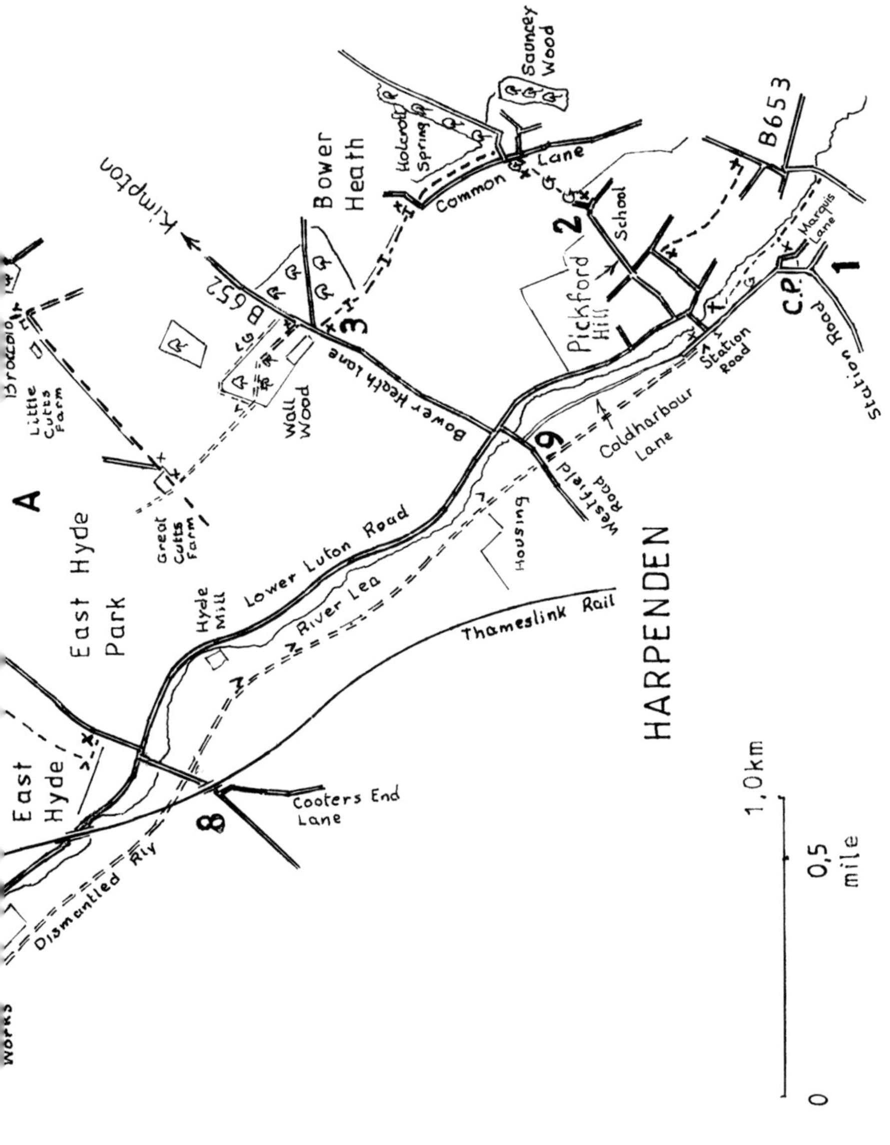

Total Distance 10.7 miles (17.3 km)
Walk A : 7.6 miles (12.3 km)
Walk B : 6.5 miles (10.5 km)

HARPENDEN, PETER'S GREEN, SOMERIES CASTLE, LEA VALLEY

WALK 7

Park in Marquis Lane car park, off Station Road, Harpenden. G.R.146,150
Parking is also possible in Coldharbour Lane nearby. G.R.143,155

Alternatively : This walk may also be completed from the N by parking at Someries Castle, G.R.119,202, starting at Item 5 and continuing to Items 6, 7, etc.

1 From the car park, cross Marquis Lane to the footpath opposite (E) into recreation ground. Follow the hedge L, do not cross the footbridge, but turn R (SE) alongside the stream L. After passing the play area R, note the weir on the River Lea. This may be seen more closely using the stepping stones. On reaching Crabtree Lane, turn L (N) and cross the river by the bridge by the ford. Continue (N) to the B653 main road and cross it into Common Lane opposite. Go past Batford Road L, then turn L (NW) onto a signed path between housing. Continue ahead with allotments R, ignoring crossing paths. At the road junction, turn R into South View Road, turn L into Roundfield Avenue, then R (NE) into Pickford Hill. Pass the school R, then turn L into Whitings Close. Go through a gate R at the end of the Close.

2 Keep to the hedge R and continue (NE) through two gates and between fences through a wooded area. Go through a further gate into Common Lane, where turn L (NW). Go past Sauncey Wood Lane R and in 20m turn R through a gap into Holcroft Spring Wood, which is carpeted with bluebells in spring. (If this access is closed, continue (NW) along Common Lane for 300m and rejoin the route at the sharp bend to the R in this lane). Keep to a well trodden path (NW) just a few metres from the road L. At a gap by a bend to the R in the road, cross the road with care to a signpost and stile opposite. Continue (NW) along a field edge with hedge R. Cross two stiles, enter a small wood and continue (NW) to Bower Heath Lane (B652) by a bungalow L.

3 Turn R along the B652 for 50m, then turn L (NW) along a signposted track through Wall Wood. Continue along this path (NW). At the intersection of paths by Great Cutts Farm, turn R (NE) and in 150m at the bend in the track, turn R then L at the signpost. With hedge L go down a track (NE) to Broccolo Cottage. Turn L passing the cottage, continue along this well-used path (N) through a wooded strip emerging at a bend in Farr's Lane. Continue (NW) along this lane for 100m, then turn R (NE) along Hyde Lane. At the road junction turn L into Peter's Green passing The Bright Star PH, R.

4 Bear L (NW) along the road to Chiltern Green, which in about 500m bends L (W). Take the next turning R (N), passing the cottages R at Chiltern Green. In about 400m at a signpost, turn L (W) into a tree-lined bridleway. This meanders through trees and is covered in bluebells in spring. After about 1km, turn L (SW) at a waymark and follow a line of trees between fields. (Note Chiltern Hall R and Luton Hoo in the distance.) At a crossing lane, turn R (W) towards a group of buildings at Someries with buildings at Luton Airport to the R. Someries Castle is worth inspection and suitable as a picnic stop.

5 Go through the kissing gate passing Someries Castle L (W), then bear R through a small meadow to another kissing gate. Go through, turn R (NW) with hedge R, and continue downhill across a field with airport R. At the airport boundary fence corner, continue downhill in the dip of the field towards houses, ignoring a path R and go under the railway bridge. Turn L (S) at the road (B653).

6 In a few metres, go through a kissing gate L signed 'Lea Valley Walk', into a narrow field. Bear L up slope through a gate onto a tarmac track (this is a multi-user path), turn R along this track. At the field end cross a by-road (Copthall Road) and continue (S) into a tree plantation, following the waymarks (S) on the course of the dismantled railway.

7 Cross the footbridge over the B653, then cross the River Lea. Pass the sewage works L, then cross the road by the former LNER station house and continue with more sewage works L. On reaching the iron bridge carrying the main line railway, continue under it down to a gate in Cooters End Lane.

8 Cross road and continue along the track of the old railway. Note the River Lea and Hyde Mill L. Follow this clear path (SE) with fence L for about 1.5km, then go up slope to Westfield Road.

9 Cross the road and continue (SE) along the path opposite until the path joins a road with housing R. Bear L at the swan waymark, then L and R into Coldharbour Lane. At All Saints Church take the path (SE) into the grounds, go pass the church and into the car park. At the gate in the corner L keep forward (SE) through a meadow by the river L. Cross through the hedge into a recreation ground, then turn sharp R to regain the car park in Marquis Lane.

Two shorter walks can also be completed as follows :

WALK A

10 Starting from the south, at Item 1, continue to Item 4. At Peter's Green, turn L along the road to Chiltern Green. Turn L (SW) along a footpath signed 'Chiltern Way', past the village hall R. At a crossing track note the housing R. Cross slightly R to a path over a stile. Cross another two stiles after the small paddock, continue (SW) with field edge L and go straight ahead at a waymark, following a line of trees L.

11 At a crossing path by a clump of trees, turn L (SE) along a clear track and in 200m turn R (SW) along a grassy path between fields. On reaching a large oak tree, turn L with housing R into Farr's Lane, where turn R (SW). At the B653 road, cross to the road almost opposite. Continue (SW) across the River Lea and at the end of the barbed wire fence L, turn L onto a tarmac track. Continue (SE) as in Item 8.

WALK B

12 Starting from the north at the car park at Someries Castle at Item 5, continue to Item 8, then turn L (NE) along the road and onto the B653. Cross with care into Farr's Lane. At the end of the housing L, turn L (NW) onto a path. After 100m by a large oak tree turn R (NE). Go uphill to a crossing track where turn L (NW). On reaching a clump of trees, go past and turn immediately R (NE) round them. Continue (NE) to the road at Peter's Green, where turn L (NW), then as in Item 4 return to Someries Castle.

Chiltern Green Farmhouse

WALK 8

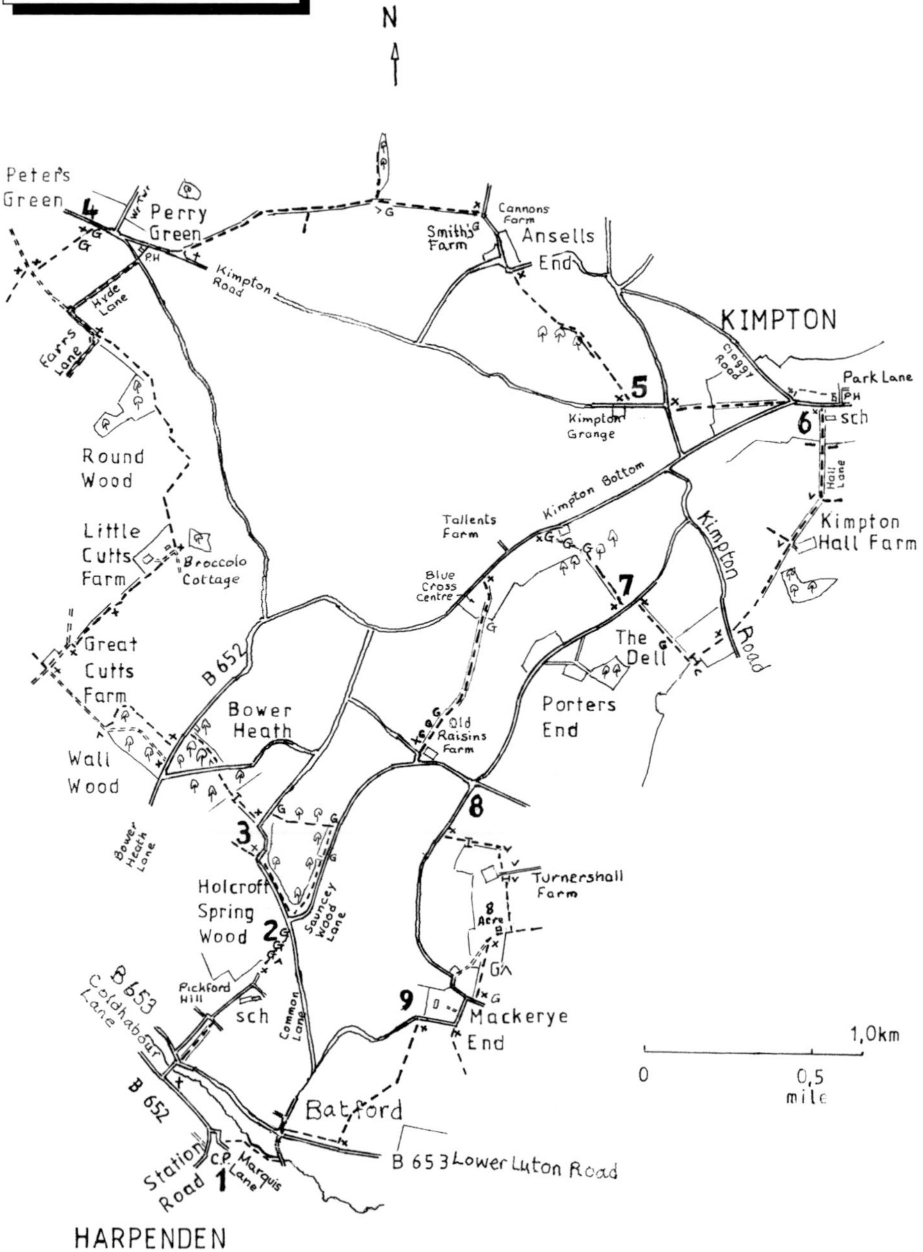

Total Distance 10.6 miles (17.0 Km)
Shorter Route 10.1 miles (16.3 km)

HARPENDEN, ANSELLS END, KIMPTON, MACKERYE END

WALK 8

Park in Marquis Lane car park, off Station Road, Harpenden. G.R.146,150
Parking is also possible in Coldharbour Lane nearby. G.R.143,155

1 From the car park, turn L and go along Station Road (NW) past All Saints Church. Turn R, cross the River Lea, and cross Lower Luton Road (B653). Immediately opposite, take the footpath (NE) between housing to Roundfield Avenue. Turn L then R (NE) up Pickford Hill passing a school R. At the bend, turn L (NE) along Whitings Close, which leads to a path (NE) through trees, pass through three gates into Common Lane.

2 Turn L (N) for a few metres, then R into Sauncey Wood Lane. Immediately bear L into the Conservancy Spinney, Holcroft Spring Wood. (If this access is closed, return to the road junction and continue for 0.5km (NW) along Common Lane. Take second signposted path L (NW) at Item 3). To continue in the wood, bear R and follow the winding path (N) parallel with Sauncey Wood Lane R, to the NE corner of the wood. Here turn L (W) along a clear track to a gate in Common Lane. Turn L along this and in 50 metres turn R (NW) along a path with hedge L.

3 Continue (NW) and cross two stiles into a wooded area. Cross the lane and follow the waymarks (NW) through trees to Bower Heath Lane (B652). Turn L (SW) along this lane and in a few metres turn R (NW) along the boundary of Wall Wood L. Turn L round the corner of the wood (SW) to a farm access road. Turn R along this road (NW). At the intersection of paths, turn R (NE), and in 150m at the bend in the track, turn R then L at the signpost. With hedge L, go down a track (NE) to 'Broccolo Cottage'. Turn L (N) round this cottage along a path between hedges for about 1.0km, emerging onto Farr's Lane. Continue (NW), and where the lane turns R, go ahead (NW) along a tarmac road. In 200m turn R (NE) at a signpost along a clear path to the water tower at Peter's Green.

4 Cross Kimpton Road, turn R along it past the Bright Star PH, R. In 400m turn L in front of the chapel. Follow the path (E) with hedge L for about 1km until reaching a wooden gate. Go through and continue (E) with hedge R, out to the road. Turn R (SE), passing Cannons Farm L at Ansells End. Where the road turns L, take the path R (SE) across a field, then with a hedge R for 800m to Kimpton Road, opposite Kimpton Grange.

5 Turn L along the road, and in 60m at the T-junction, continue (E) on the path ahead with hedge L. This runs between houses to Claggy Road near the High Street. Cross to the path opposite (NE) between houses out to Park Lane. Turn R into the High Street at The Boot PH. Turn R, and after 70m turn L along Hall Lane.

6 Continue uphill (S) towards Kimpton Hall Farm. At the farm entrance go ahead (SW) with fence L then through a gap to a road. Cross, and follow a path (SW) by a bungalow R. In 200m cross a stile, turn R (NW) along a path and with hedge L continue into a small copse. Bear L, cross the stile L (W) to a signpost R.

7 Here turn R (NW) and with hedge L continue into a small copse. Bear L, go through gate L (W), diagonally down a slope and through two more gates to the road. Turn L (SW) along Kimpton Bottom passing Tallents Farm R. At the Blue Cross Animal Centre turn L (S) along a bridleway uphill to Old Raisins Farm. At the T-junction in Sauncey Wood Lane turn L (SE) to the cross-roads.

8 Turn R (S) and in 300m turn L onto a path and continue E with hedge R. Turn R (S) round the boundary of Turnershall Farm. Cross the farm access road to the stile opposite, cross and continue (S) with hedge R over a stile to a crossing track. Turn R (W) along this into a lane at 'Eight Acre'. Continue (SW) along this lane and at 'Holly Bush Cottage', bear L (S) onto a field edge path, with fence R, behind Mackerye End Farm R to a road at a signpost. Turn R, then in 20m L (S) passing Mackerye End House R. Follow the road round the bend (W) ignoring signpost at the corner. In 150m there is a signpost L.

9 Take this path (S) between hedges, which in 0.75km emerges onto the Lower Luton Road (B653). Turn R (W) and in 250m cross the road to a thatched cottage by the small industrial estate at Batford. Cross the bridge (S) over the River Lea, then turn R (W) along the path by the river bank. At the next crossing path turn L (SW) to the car park.

Alternatively : In wet weather, you may prefer to continue along the road directly from Item 7 to Item 8 through Porter's End.

WALK 9

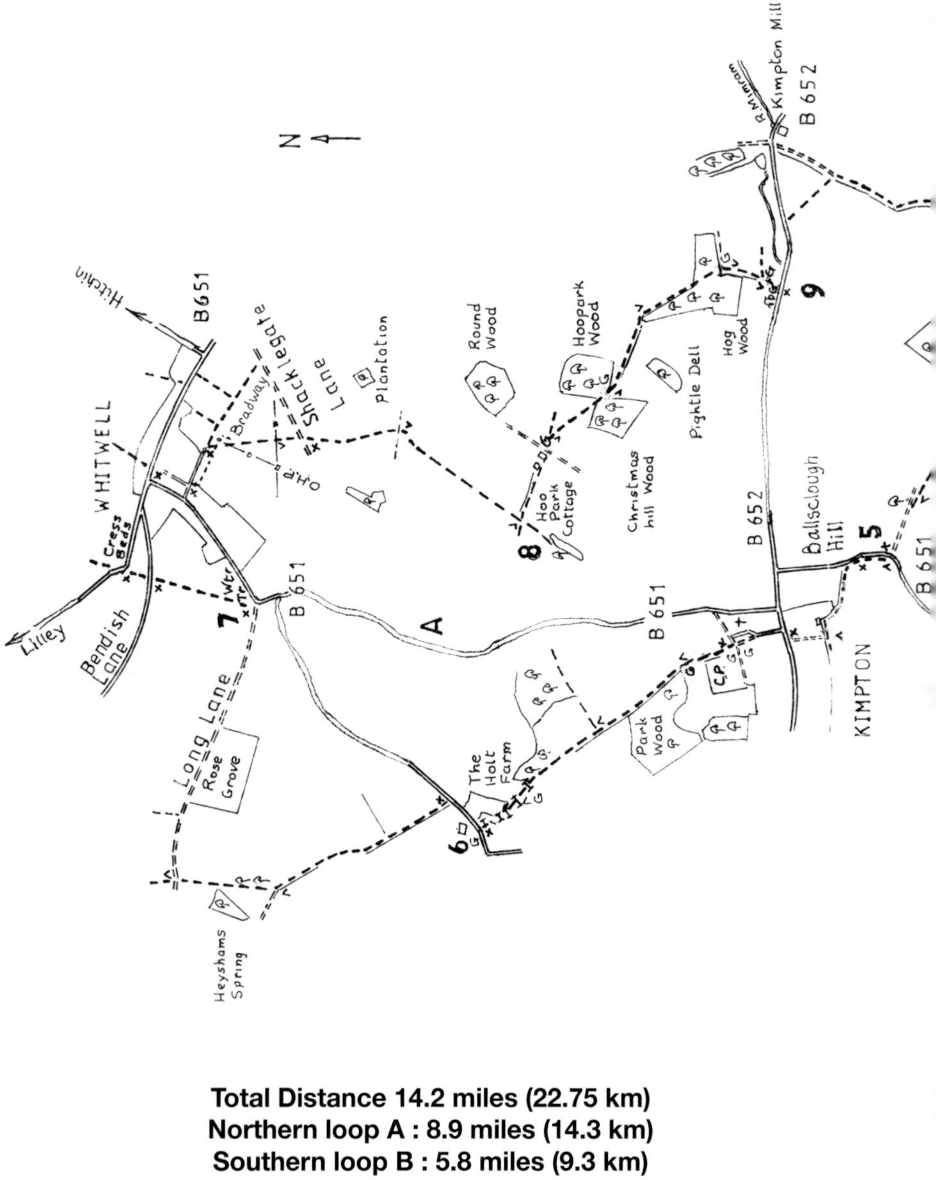

Total Distance 14.2 miles (22.75 km)
Northern loop A : 8.9 miles (14.3 km)
Southern loop B : 5.8 miles (9.3 km)

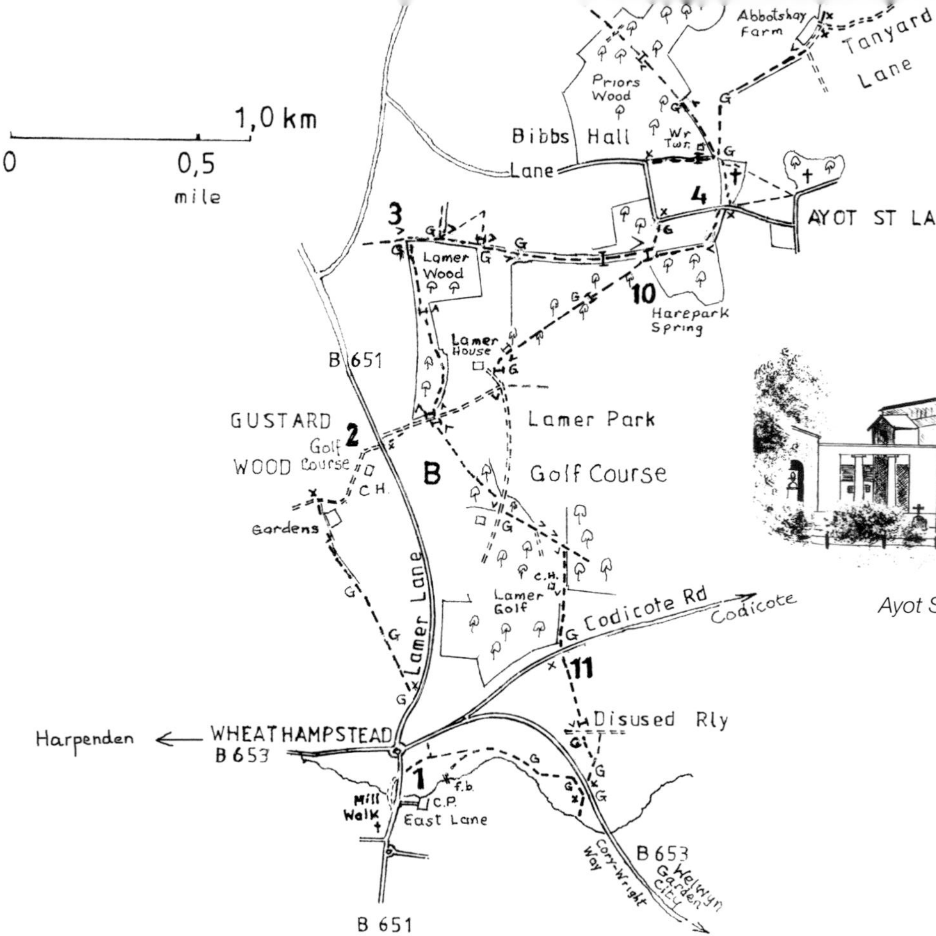

Ayot St. Lawrence Church

WHEATHAMPSTEAD, WHITWELL, AYOT ST LAWRENCE

WALK 9

Park in public car park in East Lane (beyond The Bull car park), Wheathampstead. G.R.178,141

1 From the car park return (W) to the High Street (B651). Cross the road and turn R along Mill Walk. Continue (N) to go over the roundabout into Lamer Lane (B651) and in 200m turn L through a gate at a signpost. Cross a field diagonally (NW) and follow fence R to a kissing gate. Cross a second field and go through a kissing gate onto the golf course. Continue (NW) with fence R to a crossing track by a cottage called 'Gardens'. Turn R (E), follow the track through the car park, along the private road around the clubhouse R and turn R again out to Lamer Lane.

2 Cross this road and take footpath opposite to join the private road to Lamer House (NE). In 200m cross a stile L on to a path through a wood (N). (Here are snowdrops and bluebells in season). Cross a stile in the middle of the wood. At the (NW) corner of the wood go through a kissing gate.

3 Turn R (E) and follow the edge of the wood R. Go through a kissing gate in the hedge and continue (E) along a fenced path to the (NE) corner of the wood. Turn R through a kissing gate, then L across a narrow field to a kissing gate in the fence. Continue (E) on a clear path with trees L and fence R, passing through a gate midway. Emerge at a junction of four paths and turn L (N). Continue to the corner of Bibbs Hall Lane. Bear L (N) onto the road and after 300m at a corner, turn R (E) onto a path between a fence and hedge with a wood L. Continue on this path past a small conifer plantation to emerge into a field after crossing a stile.

4 Turn L (NW) to a path with a wood L leading to a gate at the (NW) corner of the field. Enter the wood (NW) along a well-marked path to the far boundary, crossing an intermediate stile. Continue across the field (NW) towards a lone tree, onto a track. Here bear slightly L (NW) along the track to a road (B651).

5 Cross the road to steps opposite. Turn R into the field. Follow the hedge R along the field boundary downhill until past the sports pavilion R on the other side of the hedge. At a waymark, turn R (N) alongside the playing field R and emerge onto the High Street in Kimpton village. Turn R along the High Street and in 40m turn L into Church Lane. Just before this lane turns R, turn L and immediately turn R, continuing (N) across a grassy area with cottages R. Go through two gates passing car park L, and continue with fence L (N). Continue (NW), through a kissing gate, alongside Park Wood L, then a hedge L, and through a small wood to a stile at a gate. Cross a field diagonally aiming for a lone electricity pole. Go over three stiles, passing the back of The Holt Farm R, then cross a stile out to a road.

6 Turn R (NE) along this road and in 250m turn L (NW) along a signposted by-way with hedge L. Cross two large fields to a hedge gap. After 20m, turn R to continue along the by-way (N) with a short line of trees R. Continue across a field passing near to the corner of a small wood L, then (N) to a crossing track called Long Lane. Turn R (E) along it, go past Rose Grove wood R, until reaching Whitwell water tower on the corner of the B651.

7 At the tower turn L (N) down a by-way and cross Bendish Lane to the next road. Turn R (E) along this road into Whitwell, noting the watercress beds L. Opposite a cul-de-sac, The Valley, turn R into Buttons Lane and go up Oldfield Rise to Bradway. Turn L then R into the recreation ground car park. On entering turn L (SE) through a hedge gap on a bridleway with housing L. At a waymark bear R (S) across a field under power lines towards a mast. Cross a track and continue (S) down a slope to a waymarked gap in the hedge. Go up the slope bearing R (SW) and in 600m go through another hedge gap to a waymarked path junction.

8 Turn L (E) with hedge L towards a large barn and meet a private road at Hoo Park Cottage. Turn L for 20m to a kissing gate R. Go through this and bear R (SE) diagonally across a field to a gate in the middle of a line of trees, Hoopark Wood. Go through, bear L and continue with wood L and then trees R to the northern tip of Hog Wood. At the far side of this turn R (SE) alongside the wood R, through a wood, and bear R downhill (S) with hedge R to a kissing gate in a field corner. Turn R through this gate, then bear L over a footbridge to another kissing gate into Kimpton Road (B652).

9 Turn L (E) with care along this busy road for 350m. Just after a double bend turn R (SE) up a farm track. At the top of the hill go through a hedge gap to a crossing track. Turn R (S) onto a path with hedge R. The path soon goes up between hedges and leads to Abbotshay and Tanyard Lane. Turn R into the lane and just beyond the farm at the bend take the path R (SW) with hedge L. At the field corner go through a gate and go diagonally (S) across a field to another gate by Ayot Church. Go through and turn R (S) and along the rear of the church to Bibbs Hall Lane. Turn R (W) along this lane and in 40m enter a field (SW) at Priors Holt. Continue with hedge L and go down steps to a crossing track in a wood, Harepark Spring. Turn R (W) along this to the junction of four paths.

10 Bear L (SW) along the avenue of lime trees, cross a stile, then with golf course L, continue and cross another stile to meet the private road at Lamer Park Farm gateway. Bear L (S) on this road for only 100m and continue ahead (S) when the road goes R. Continue with high wire fence and golf course L. Turn L through a large metal gate 60m after beginning of woodland L and R. Continue (SE) through trees with golf course L and R. Bear L towards a line of pines, past the club house and car park R. Continue (S) alongside the golf club access road, crossing it by the waymark, and continue along the grass verge to a kissing gate onto Codicote Road.

11 Cross this road and follow a signposted track (S). Cross a stile and the disused railway cutting, go up the bank opposite through a gate (S) into a field. Continue across this field to another gate. Continue (S) through a wooded strip into a lane. Turn R along this lane which goes under the Cory-Wright Way. In 40m turn sharp R (NW) through a gate along a bridleway parallel to and above the lane. Go through a gate and turn L between fences. Continue (W) through another gate, noting views of the River Lea. Leave the bridleway by bearing L through a hedge gap onto a permissive path following the river bank. Cross the footbridge, turn R into Meads Lane, then bear R into East Lane and car park R.

Alternatively : This walk can be completed in shorter loops A and B, starting at Item 4. Only limited roadside parking is available at Ayot St Lawrence, G.R.195,168.

Kimpton Church

WALK 10

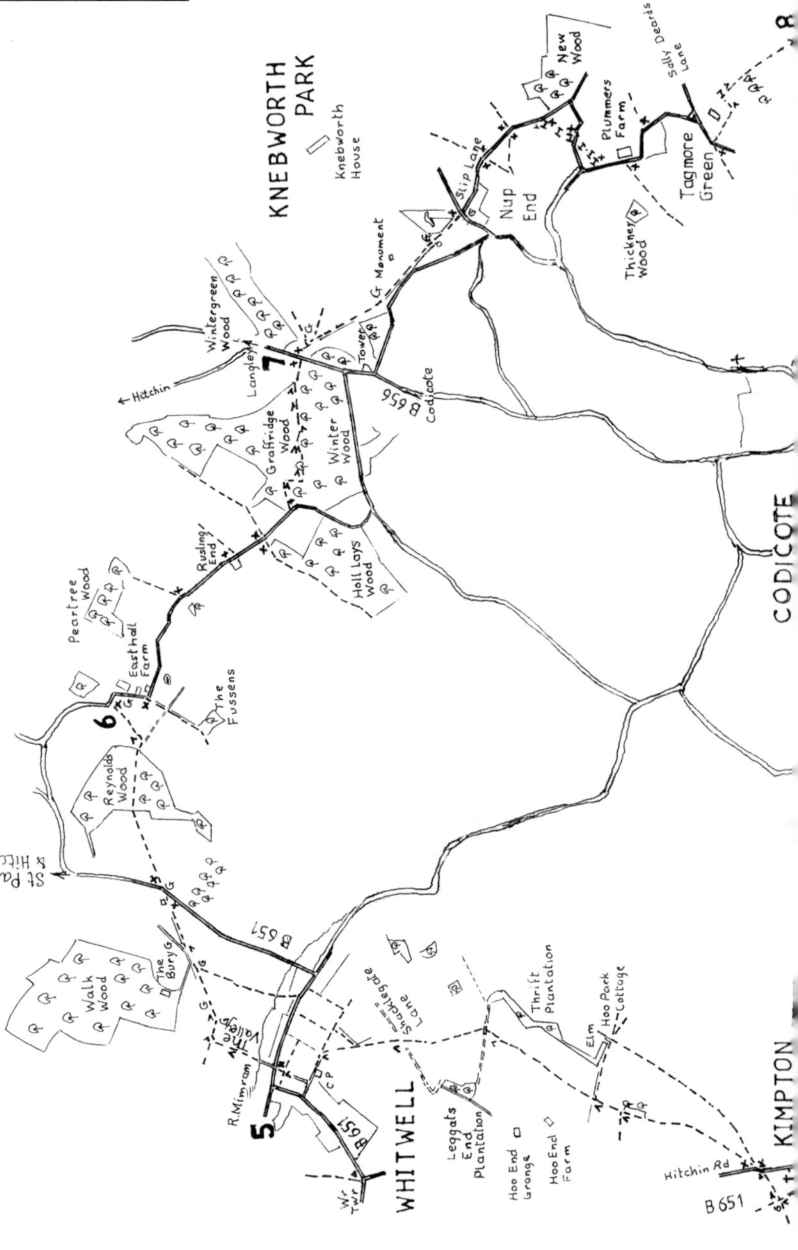

Total Distance 13.5 miles (21.7 km)

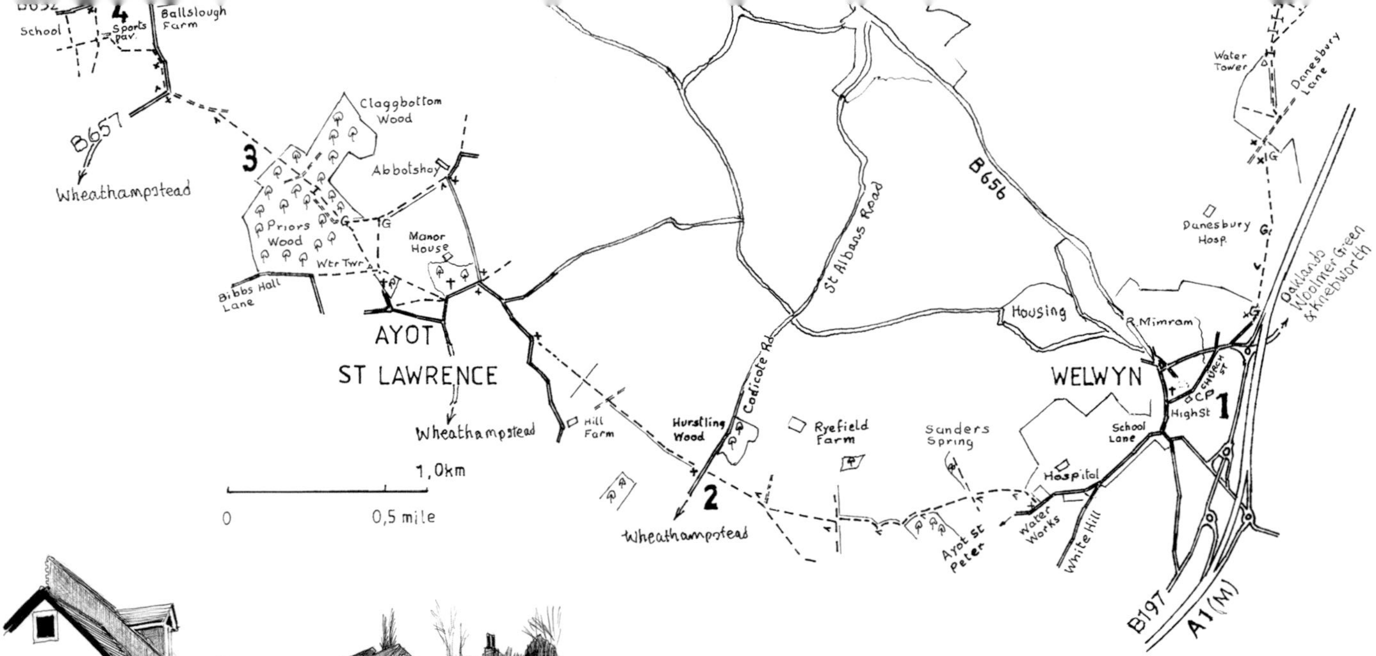

School
4
Sports pav.
Ballslough Farm
B657
Wheathampstead
3
Claggbottom Wood
Abbotshay
Priors Wood
Wtr Twr
Manor House
Bibbs Hall Lane
AYOT
ST LAWRENCE
Wheathampstead
Hill Farm
1,0km
0
0,5 mile
St Albans Road
Codicote Rd
B656
Hurstling Wood
2
Wheathampstead
Ryefield Farm
Sanders Spring
Ayot St Peter
Water Works
White Hill
Hospital
School Lane
High St
CP
Church St
1
WELWYN
Housing
R. Mimram
Danesbury Hosp.
Water Tower
Danesbury Lane
Oaklands Woolmer Green & Knebworth
B197
A1(M)

Welwyn

WELWYN, KIMPTON, WHITWELL, KNEBWORTH PARK

WALK 10

Park in public car park in Church Street, Welwyn. G.R.233,162

1 From the car park, turn L (SW) into Church Street to St Mary's Church. At the T-junction turn L (S) along the High Street. Turn R (SW) into School Lane. At the fork in the road, ignore White Hill L and continue R (W) along the road towards Ayot St Peter, past the hospital, water works, and electricity plant R. At the end of the iron railings, turn R (NW) at the signpost, climb the bank and follow the fence R to the corner. Turn L (W) and aim for the trees in the distance; cross the farm track. Continue across the field then alongside trees and hedge L (W). Go through the hedge gap, turn R (NW) then follow round the field edge with hedge R. Continue through a second hedge gap; cross the field (W) into a bridleway and bear R (NW) down to the Codicote Road.

2 Cross the road at the signpost and follow the bridleway with hedge L (NW). Cross the track leading to Hill Farm and continue (NW) across the field to the road. Turn R (NW) along the road. Ignore the road off to the R. After a further 150m enter the bridleway R (N) by the signpost; go past The Manor House L, to Abbotshay. Turn L (SW) at the signpost, then with hedge L continue to a gate. Go through and turn R (W) with woodland R to a gate in the corner of the wood. Enter the wood and go firstly (W), then (NW) along a well-marked path to the far boundary, crossing an intermediate stile.

3 Continue across the field (NW) towards a lone tree, onto a track. Here bear slightly L (NW) along the track to a road. Cross the road with care to steps opposite. Turn R into the field. Follow the hedge R along the field boundary until past the large sports pavilion R on the other side of the hedge. At a waymark, turn R (N) alongside the playing field R and emerge onto the High Street in Kimpton.

4 Turn R along the High Street and in 40m turn L into Church Lane. Continue (N) up the hill past the church (R) onto a path bearing L between cottages. At the last cottage L, turn R (NW) and after 20m turn R again (NE). Go parallel to the lane on a grassy track past the redbrick cottage R and alongside a wall R out to the B651. Turn L up this road for 30m to the signpost R. Enter the private road R and in 30m bear L along the path running diagonally across the field (NE) aiming for the L edge of the copse in the distance. Go alongside this copse (NE) to a gap in a crossing hedge. Go through and continue (NE) straight across the next field down to a waymarked gap in the hedge. Bear L (N) uphill. Cross the farm track called Shacklegate Lane. Continue (N) towards housing and into Bradway at Whitwell. Turn L, passing Whitwell recreation ground car park L. Turn R (N) down Oldfield Rise and follow the track between housing to Buttons Lane and down to Whitwell High Street.

5 Cross the road and go down The Valley (NE). Cross the River Mimram and continue up to a track. Bear R (E) at the T-junction and in 100m enter a field R at a kissing gate. Go diagonally (NE) 20m and through the left-hand gate. Continue (NE) across the field to a metal kissing gate. Go forward onto a drive that curves L ahead and in 40m go R through a kissing gate. Bear L (NE) down across a meadow towards a lodge at the corner of a walled garden. Go through a metal kissing gate and trees to the road. Turn L and in 30m turn R at a signpost up a track, with hedge L, into Reynolds Wood. Continue (E) through the wood. At the end of the wood, go ahead with hedge L for 50m. Turn L across a field (NE), go through a gate by farm buildings R and continue straight ahead 50m to a road.

6 Turn R (SE) along this road and follow round Easthall Farm L. Continue (SE) along this road (past three signposts L) to the boundary of Graffridge Wood. At a signpost turn L (E) into the wood on a forest track. After 150m, turn R (SE) onto a narrower track, which is well waymarked, until it emerges onto the B656 road. Cross to a signpost opposite. Bear R to go through a tall metal kissing gate to enter Knebworth Park.

7 Follow the fence R (SE), going through one intermediate tall metal kissing gate and one more tall metal kissing gate to exit the Park. Follow the path, through a kissing gate and bear L to a gate onto the road at Nup End. Cross and continue opposite (SE) along Slip Lane for 700m. 70m before the wood boundary L, take the signposted path R (SW) through the hedge gap. Turn L, cross a stile and head diagonally across the field (SW), crossing three more stiles. Cross a lane and a stile and again head diagonally across the field (SW). crossing two more stiles to join another lane. Turn L (S) along the lane, going past Plummer's Farm L, to Tagmore Green. At the T-junction turn R (SW) along the road. In 200m at a signpost turn L (SE) leaving the road. Continue between two fences to a corner. Turn L (NE) and in 100m turn R; go over a stile into a field.

8 Continue (SE) across this field and cross the left-hand stile. Continue with hedge R to a field corner. Turn R (S) over a stile. Continue towards the water tower, crossing three more stiles. Go past the tower R and continue (S) straight ahead along a track and then a footpath to a T-junction. Turn L (SE) along a lane and in 40m turn R (S) along a road for 100m. At the signpost L go through a kissing gate (S) and down the slope towards Welwyn. Continue (S), going through two kissing gates and emerge into a lane. At a T-junction, turn R and cross the road. Turn L into Church Street and continue downhill to the car park L.

Spanish Chesnut
in Knebworth Park

24 FOOTPATH WALKS IN HERTFORDSHIRE

The Bury, King's Walden - Walk 2

The George & Dragon Codicote

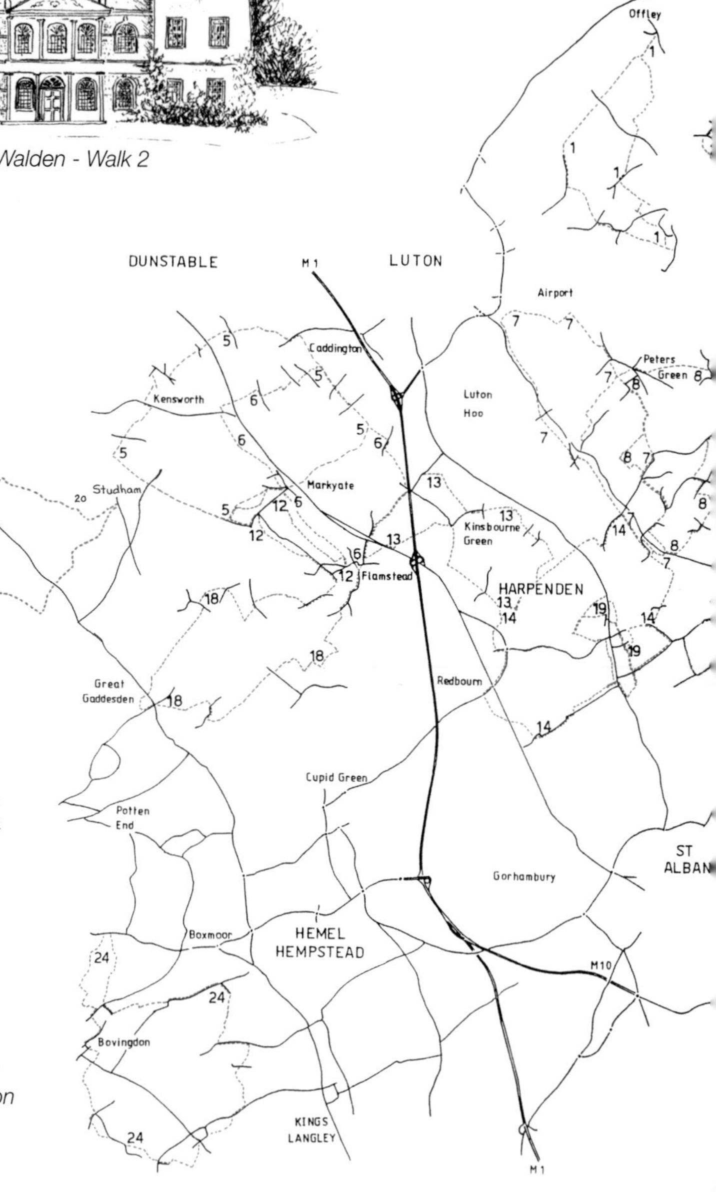

Minsden Chapel - Walk 3

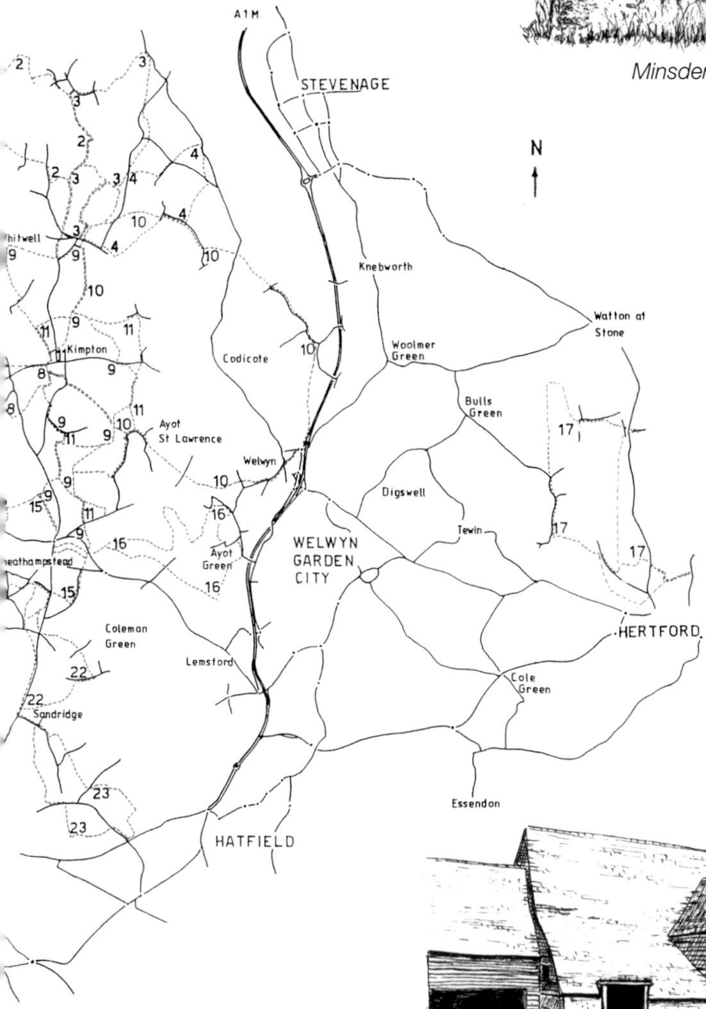

Kimpton Hall Farm - Walk 8

WALK 11

Kimpton Hall Farm

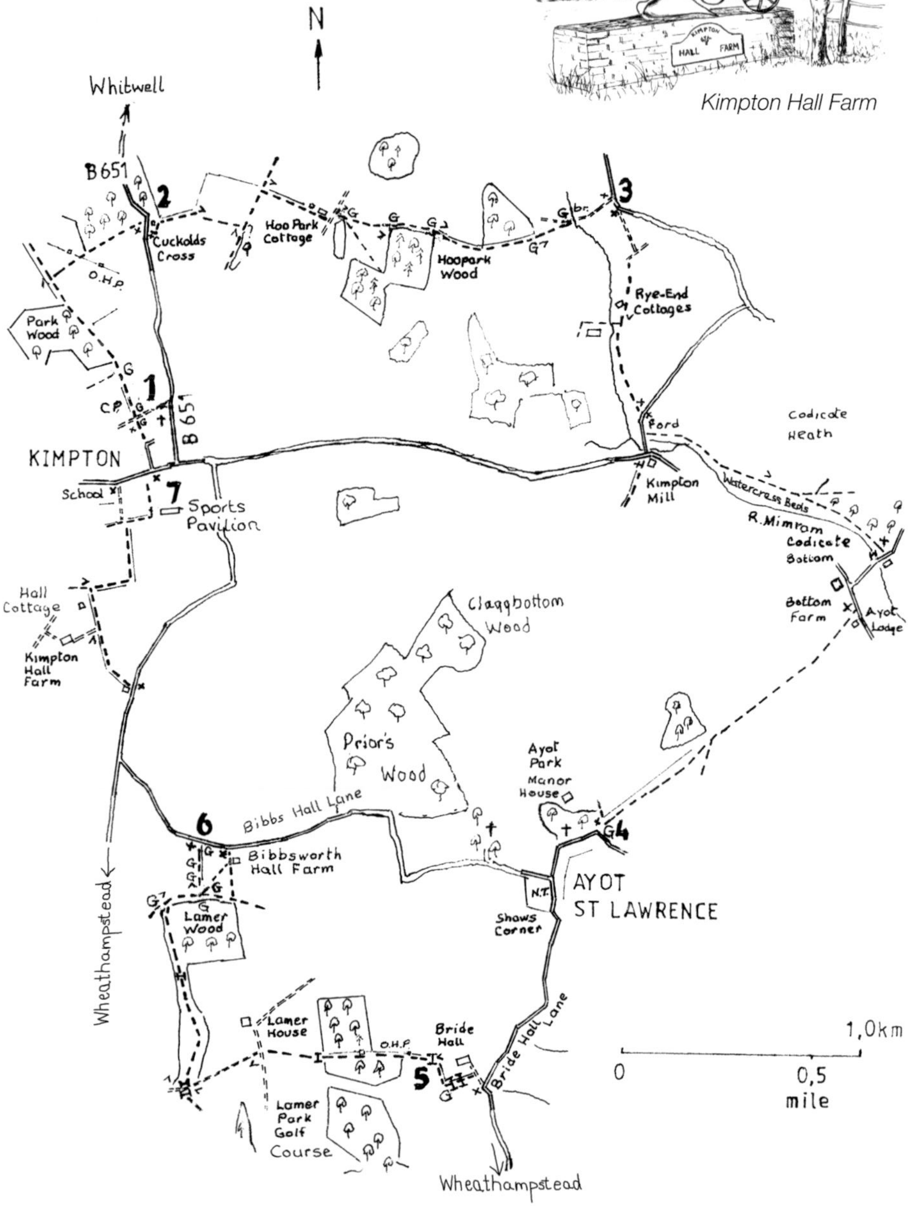

Total Distance 8.4 miles (13.5 km)

KIMPTON, AYOT ST LAWRENCE, LAMER PARK

WALK 11

Park in Kimpton recreation ground car park behind the Church, off the B651 Hitchin Road. G.R.176,186

1 Turn L out of car park through a gate and go up the field path (N) with fence L. Go through the kissing gate, continue (NW) with Park Wood L, then 140m after the end of the wood, turn R along a grass track (NE). Cross under a power line, continue with woodland L and go out to the road at Cuckolds Cross.

2 At the road turn R and in 20m at a signpost turn L. Walk alongside a garden hedge, then continue with a field hedge L (E) at first, then bear (NE). At the waymark, turn R (E) across the field to the L corner of a small group of trees. Here turn L (N) along the track and in 150m turn R (E) with hedge L, passing the large barn, and meet a private road at Hoo Park Cottages. Turn L for 20m to a kissing gate R. Go through this and continue straight across the field (E), ignoring the diagonal path (SE), to reach a kissing gate at the corner of Hoopark Wood R. Continue (E) alongside this wood R. At the far corner of this wood go through a kissing gate and continue (E) with hedge L. Soon the path leads to another wood L with a kissing gate at the far corner. Go straight down the field ahead to a kissing gate into a driveway. Bear R along this drive, cross the bridge over the River Mimram to the road.

3 Turn R (S) along this road and in 30m bear R at the bridleway sign. Continue past Rye-End Cottages R and along track to farm R, along the river valley to meet a lane at a bend. Bear R (S), pass watercress beds R and turn L (SE) onto a bridleway to Codicote Bottom. Turn R on meeting the road. Proceed with care along this road to a T-junction. Here turn L, then in 100m, by Ayot Lodge, turn R (SW) uphill on a farm track. Where this farm track bends R, leave it to continue ahead with fence R. Go through a kissing gate and turn L onto a driveway leading to a road at Ayot St Lawrence.

4 At this road turn R (SW), pass the ruined church R and follow the road round L to Shaw's Corner, a National Trust property, ignoring the road R. Continue along the road (S) for 900m to Bride Hall R. At the signpost turn R through a pedestrian wicket gate L set into the main security gate, and go up the gravel drive for 50m. At the corner of the barn turn L (W) through a gate, pass the large ornamental gates R and follow the brick wall R to a stile. Cross this and continue with wall R, to another stile at the far corner. Cross, turn R (NW) onto a hedged path. After this bends L, cross a stile next to a gate R onto a fenced and hedged track.

5 Continue (W) through woodland. Cross the stile and continue across the golf course into the private road near Lamer House. Bear L, then follow this tarmac road (SW), with hedge R, until reaching Lamer Wood. Turn R over a stile onto a path through this wood (N). (Here are snowdrops and bluebells in season). Cross a stile in the middle of the wood. At the (NW) corner of the wood go through a kissing gate. Turn R (E) and follow the edge of the wood R. In 200m turn L (N), just before a kissing gate. Keeping hedge R, go through three gates, passing farm buildings R, then through another gate into Bibbs Hall Lane.

6 Turn L (NW) to a T-junction at which turn R. In 300m turn L (N) onto a signed track to Kimpton Hall Farm. When the track goes L, continue ahead with hedge L on a concrete track to a crossing hedge. Turn R (E) alongside this hedge R to the corner of the field. Turn L (N) with hedge R. At the crossing path, turn R and in 130m turn L (N) alongside the playing field R and emerge onto the High Street, Kimpton.

7 Turn R along the High Street and in 40m turn L (N) into Church Lane. Just before this lane turns R, turn L at the gap into Garden Fields. Immediately turn R and continue (N) across a grassy area with cottages R. Go through a gate and turn L into the car park.

WALK 12

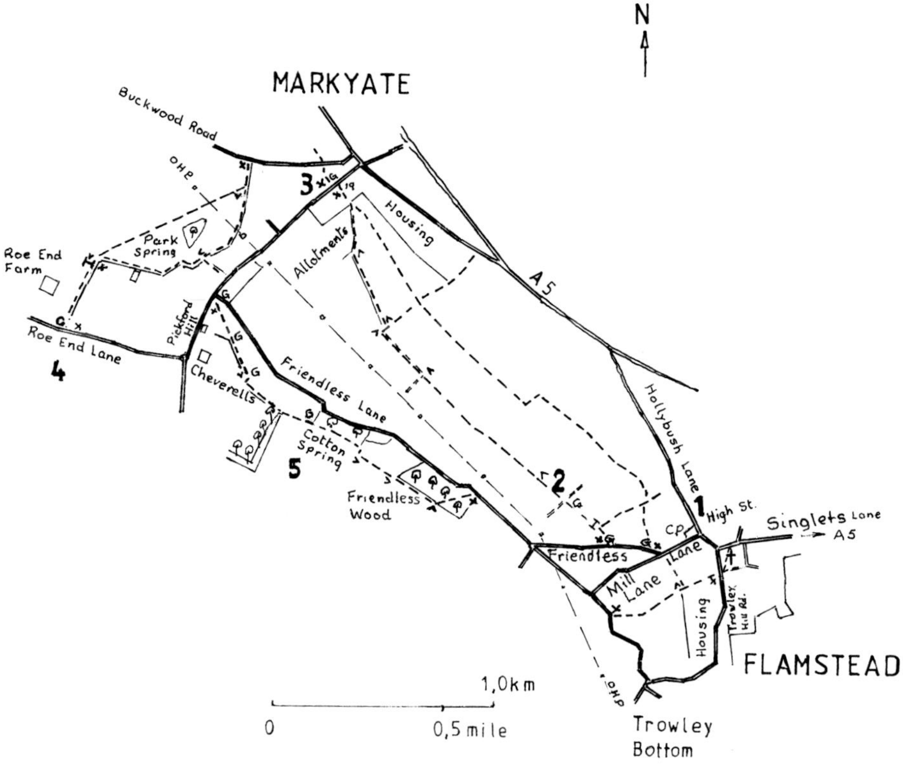

High Street, Markyate

Total Distance 5.3 miles (8.5 km)

FLAMSTEAD, MARKYATE, CHEVERELLS

WALK 12

Park in Flamstead recreation ground car park at the junction of Friendless Lane and Hollybush Lane. G.R.077,147

NOTE : The walk is marked by 'Herts Way' signs from the start to Item 4.

1 On leaving the car park turn R into Friendless Lane and continue along it, bearing R (W) at junction with Mill Lane. In about 200m at the second footpath sign R, go through a kissing gate. Follow the fence R (NW) to a gate. Continue (NW) with hedge R to a kissing gate, then across the field to a second gate.

2 Cross the farm track and continue (NW) through a hedge into a large field. Go ahead (NW) across it aiming for the 6th pylon ahead. The target, a hedge corner, will soon become visible in the distance. At this corner a clear track continues (NW) with hedge L. Follow round a short R and L to allotments. Keep to the allotments' fence L. Take the L fork downhill to the road alongside No.19 at bottom R.

3 Turn L (W) along the road and in 30m turn R (NW) through metal gates. Cross a road, then on a path through housing, past the Baptist Church, then out to Buckwood Road. Turn L (W) and in 350m reach the end of the housing L. At the signpost marked 'Roe End Lane', turn L (S) and go uphill with hedge and housing L towards a power pylon L. Follow round the field corners (W). At a three-way path junction turn L (S) and go through gap. Continue alongside a hedge L, past Roe End Farm R. This leads to a gate into Roe End Lane.

4 Turn L (E) along this lane for 600m to a T-junction opposite a house called 'Cheverells'. Turn L (NE) along Pickford Hill and in 300m turn R (SE) onto a road signposted 'Bamstead'. In 20m turn R through a signed swing gate. Continue (SE) diagonally across a field to a second gate. In a further 300m go through a third gate with fence R. Continue (S) at the end of a woodland strip R, go across a field (SE) to another gate to a wood called Cotton Spring.

5 Continue forward with wood L, follow round a short R and L; do not turn towards farm buildings, but follow the waymark ahead (SE). Continue with hedge L then the boundary of Friendless Wood L. Ignore entrance to wood L, pass DEFRA sign R and in a further 200m at a waymark, turn L (E) on a path through the wood to Friendless Lane (see note below). Turn R along the lane (SE). At the crossroads go ahead under the power line. Pass another road junction L and as the road begins to go downhill, turn L (E) at a footpath sign. Continue (E) across a field towards Flamstead Church, then on a path between housing for 200m to Trowley Hill Road. Cross road and go through churchyard. Turn L onto road at The Spotted Dog PH. Turn R at T-junction into Chapel Road, continue ahead 150m to car park.

NOTE : A Mr Frindles owned land in this area in the mid 19th century. It seems likely the writing of this name became corrupted to 'Friendless'.

End wall of a cottage, Markyate

WALK 13

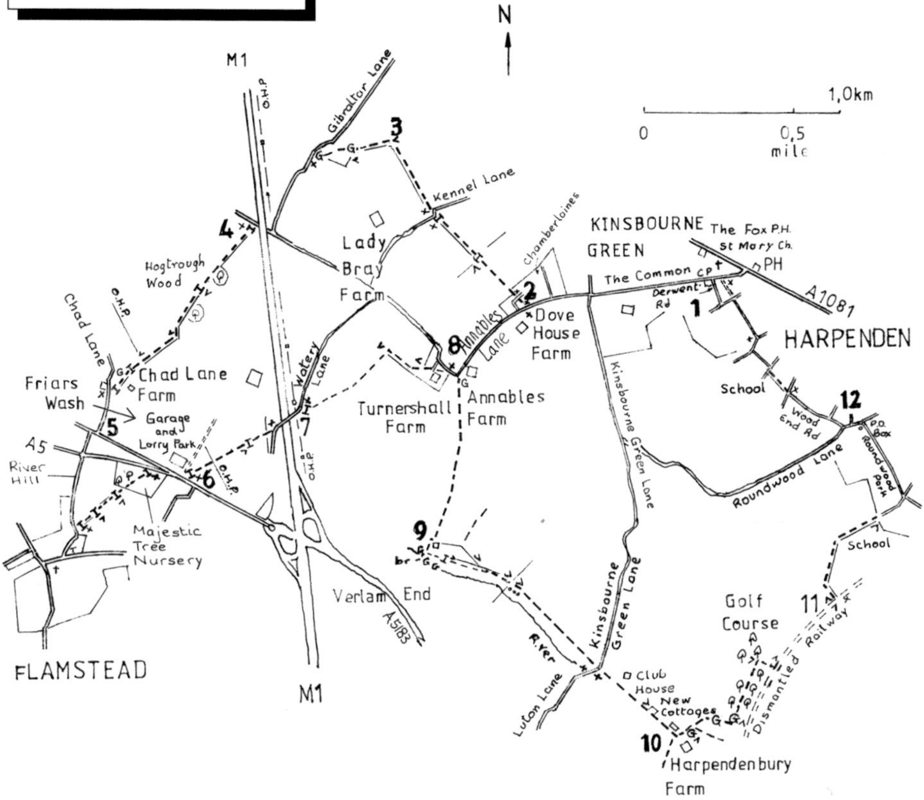

Turnershall Farm

Total Distance 8.4 miles (13.5 km)
Shorter route 8.0 miles (12.9 km)

KINSBOURNE GREEN & FLAMSTEAD — Walk 13

*Since publication, the permissive route from Annables Farm **(8)** to Verlam End **(9)** has been withdrawn; please replace **Items 5 – 9** with the following revised text & map. Total distance 8.4 miles (13.5km).* <u>*Do not take **Alternative** shorter route at Friars Wash*</u>.

5 Turn R (NW) along Old Watling Street and in 10m turn L (S) down to the A5. Cross with care and continue (S) up River Hill to T-junction with Flamstead High Street/Singlets Lane. *(Here are interesting almshouses, a church, and inns providing food).*

6 Turn L, pass shop/post office L, continuing along Singlet Lane. At bend in road, turn R into Delmerend Lane and almost immediately take footpath L to Norringtonend Farm. Continue along path and downhill, go through two gates either side of a track, through a 3rd gate, and up to 4th gate in LH corner of field and Lower Sawpit Wood R.

7 Bear R uphill towards Norringtonend Farm. At the top, go over stile, keeping farm on L. In a short distance, turn L, go through gate into Redding Lane, where turn R. Cross bridge over motorway and immediately turn L. Go through two gates. Bear R and follow Herts Showground fence R downhill to gate onto Dunstable Road (A5183) opposite Watling House.

8 Cross the road with care, turn L and follow pavement towards the M1. Just before the motorway, take footpath R, through gate and over stile. Skirt field L, then take path R to Verlam End, where turn R onto farm track to go round edge of garden L.

9 Cross bridge over River Ver, turn R (E) and into field, continue (SE) to meet hedge L. Continue (SE) with hedge L. At a crossing hedge near beehives, continue ahead (SE) aiming for a group of trees just to L of a building with a single chimney stack. Cross the road to the bridleway opposite. Continue (SE) passing Redbourn Golf Clubhouse and 'New Cottages' L.

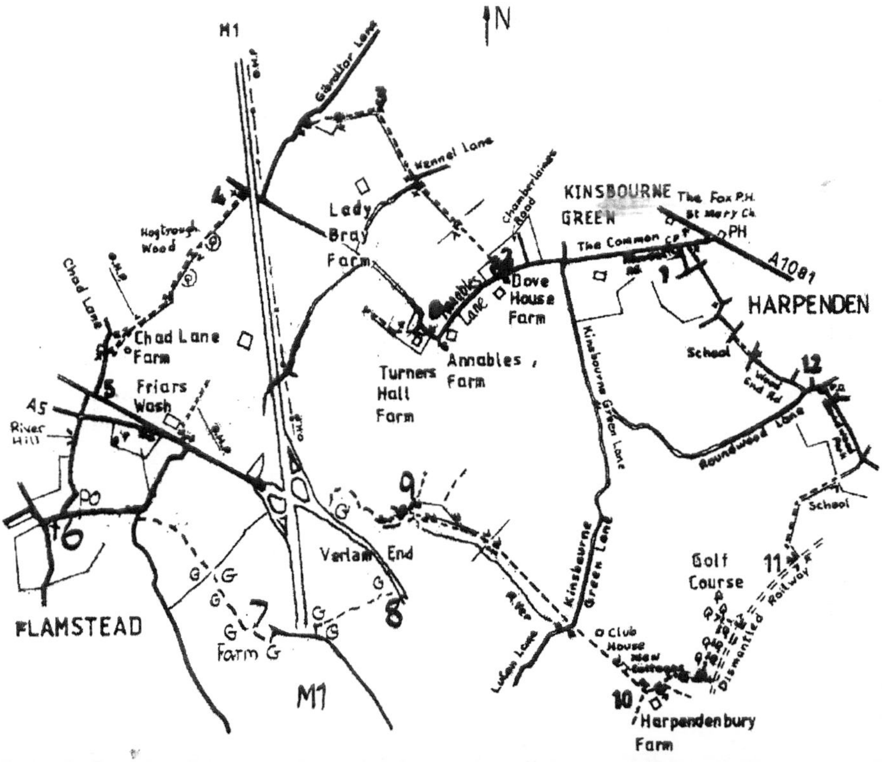

KINSBOURNE GREEN, FLAMSTEAD, ANNABLES

WALK 13

Park at Kinsbourne Green, near Derwent Road junction with The Common and Luton Road. G.R.113,160

1 From the road junction, walk (W) along 'The Common' on grassy verge L past attractive houses. Cross Kinsbourne Green Lane. Continue (W) past Chamberlaines R and in 200m turn R (NW) along a path between gardens.

2 Beyond these gardens continue (NW) on a grassy track, over a stile in a crossing wire fence. Continue (NW) with wire fence L, cross a stile into Kennel Lane. Turn R and immediately L at the signpost along a path with hedge L (NW). In about 400m at a hedge corner turn L (W).

3 Follow the ditch L along the field edge, go through a gate into a meadow. Go diagonally R (W) aiming to the L of the power pylon. Go through a gate into Gibraltar Lane and turn L (SW). At the end of the lane, turn R and go under the motorway.

4 On emerging from the underpass, climb the roadside bank L, cross the stile and continue (SW) with wire fence L. Go past Hogtrough Wood L, follow the hedge or fence L, go under the power line into a paddock. Cross the stile into Chad Lane by the farm, turn L and go down to the end of the lane.

5 Turn R (NW) along Old Watling Street and in 10m turn L (S) down to the A5. Cross with care and continue (S) up River Hill into Flamstead village. Here are interesting almshouses, a church, also inns providing food. To continue, retrace your steps down the lane (N) by the telephone box. Cross the stile R by the allotments and continue (NE) with hedge R. In 100m cross a stile with wood L. Continue along a field edge to another stile. Cross stile into Majestic Tree Nursery and follow waymarked path to finger post and stile visible on the A5. Turn R along the A5.

6 Proceed (SE) along the A5 for 150m past a garage forecourt and a lorry park L. Cross the road at the bollards, turn R, cross the lorry park exit to the embankment, turn L to the stile and signpost 50m ahead. Cross the field (NE), heading just to R of the power pylon. Cross another stile, continue (NE) through the fence gap onto Watery Lane bridge and over the MI.

7 At the far end of the bridge, cross the stile R into a field. Follow path (NE) across the field. At the hedge corner waymark, turn (SE) and follow hedge R towards the large brick barn. Continue (E) past farm R, cross the farm access road and paddock to signpost in Annables Lane.

8 In a few metres where the lane turns L, turn R (S) through metal gates to a farm track. Ignoring crossing path, continue along a broad gravel track (S).

9 Go past Verlam End and just before the bridge over the River Ver, turn L (E) and through three large wooden gates. Cross the stable yard and the stile ahead into a field, continue (SE) to meet the hedge L. Continue (SE) with hedge L. At a crossing hedge near the beehives, continue ahead (SE) aiming for a group of trees just to L of a building with a single chimney stack. Cross the road to the bridleway opposite. Continue (SE) passing Redbourn Golf Clubhouse and 'New Cottages' L.

10 Pass a large barn L and just in front of the entrance to Harpendenbury Farm, turn L (NE) past a barn R. Where the track turns R, go forwards (NE) through a gate into a paddock. Go (NE) through another gate and a third turning L (N) into a woodland with golf course L. On emerging from the wood, turn R (E) at the waymark keeping to the edge of the golf course R. In about 100m turn sharp R (E) and go through a gap. In a further 50m at a T-junction with the 'Nicky Line', a disused railway track, turn L (NE) along it. In about 450m at the pipe rail barrier turn L (NW) at a waymark.

11 Bear R, pass a gated paddock and continue (N) past Roundwood School R between housing. At the first cross-roads, turn L (NW) along Roundwood Park. Ignore side roads, continue to a post box at a T-junction. Turn L (W) into Roundwood Lane, then the second turning R (NW) into Wood End Road.

12 Continue to Wood End School, then (NW) along a path with the school boundary L. At the T-junction turn R into Tuffnells Way, then L into Crosspaths. Turn R into Shepherds Way. At the bend in the road keep forward (N) along a path between housing to meet the Common, turn L for the car park.

Alternatively : If you do not wish to visit Flamstead village at Item 5, turn L along Old Watling Street directly to the garage at Item 6.

WALK 14

Harpendenbury Farm

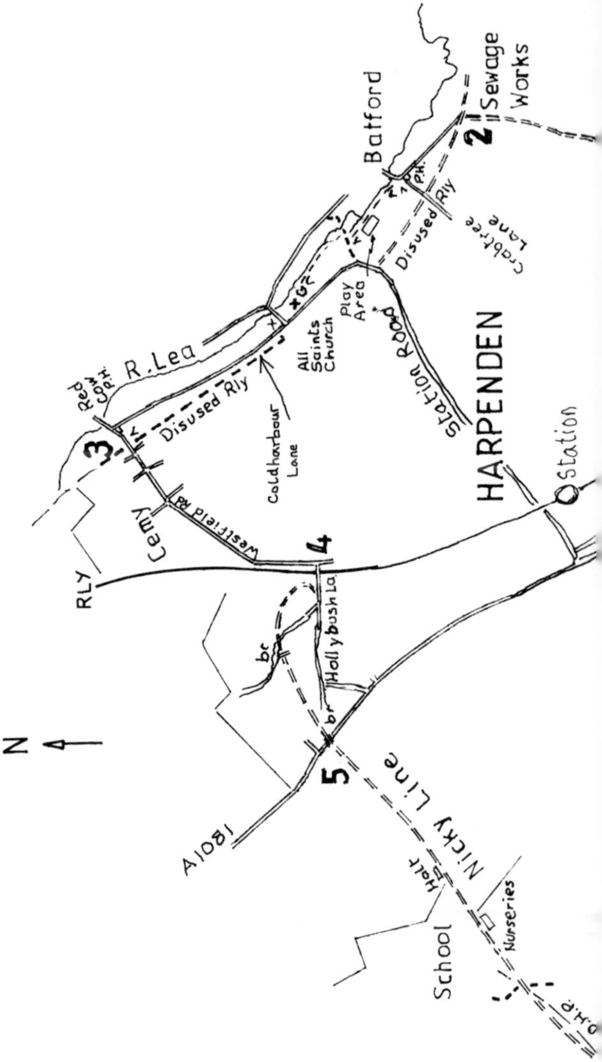

Total Distance 11.2 miles (17.8 km)

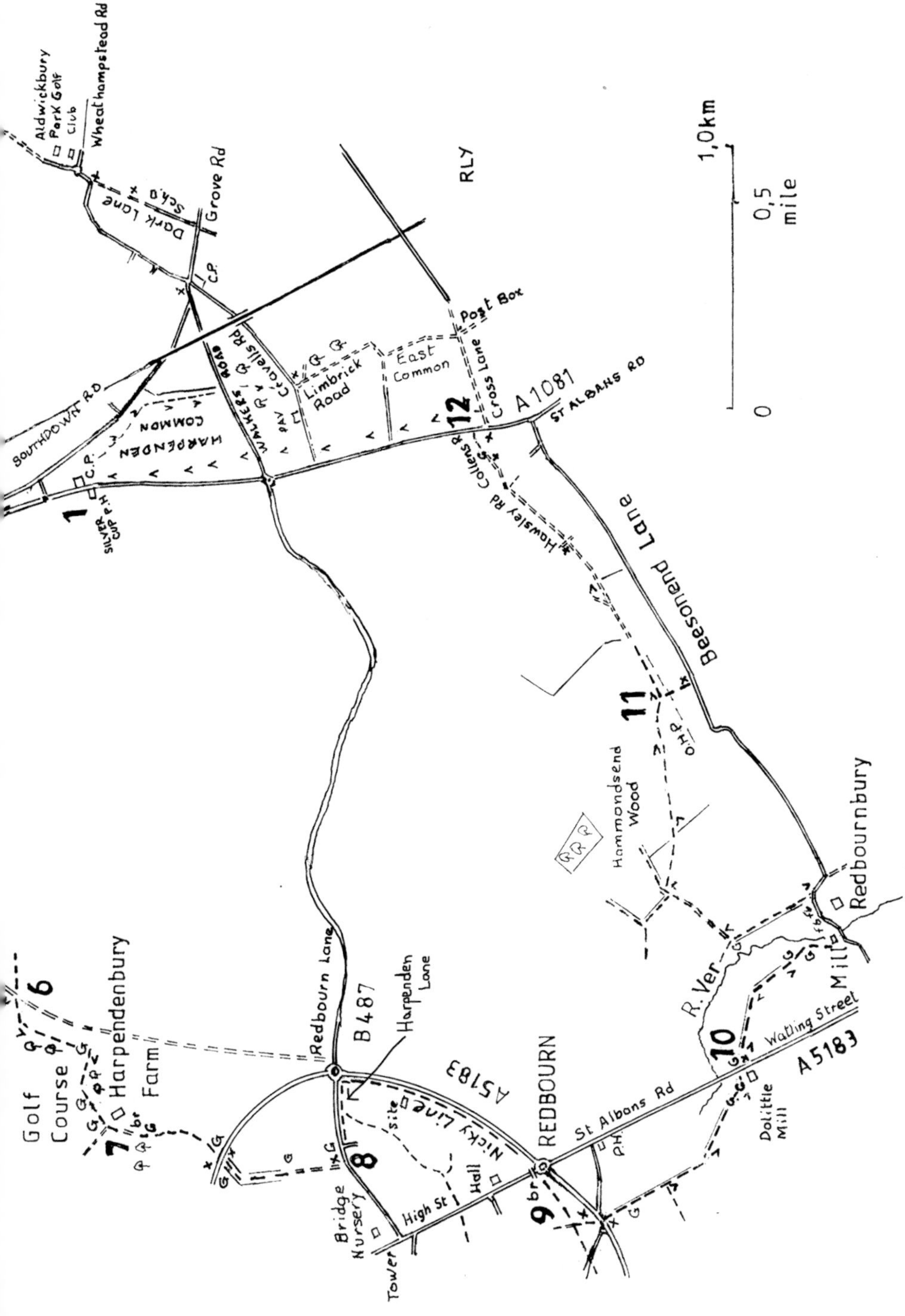
Aldwickbury Park Golf Club
Wheathampstead Rd
Dark Lane
Sch.o.
Grove Rd
C.P.
RLY
Post Box
SOUTHDOWN RD
HARPENDEN COMMON
WALKERS ROAD
Cravells Rd
PAV
Limbrick Road
East Common
Cross Lane
12
A1081
ST ALBANS RD
Collens Rd
Hawsley Rd
1
SILVER CUP P.H.
C.P.
Beesonend Lane
11
O.H.P.
Hammondsend Wood
Redbournbury
R. Ver
Mill
Watling Street
A5183
10
Dolittle Mill
REDBOURN
St Albans Rd
P.H.
9
br
Hall
High St
Bridge Nursery
Tower
8
site
Nicky Line
A5183
Harpenden Lane
B487
Redbourn Lane
6
Harpendenbury Farm
Golf Course
7
0
0,5 mile
1,0km

CIRCULAR WALK AROUND HARPENDEN

WALK 14

Part of Lea Valley Walk and the Nicky Line

Park on Harpenden Common on the A1081, opposite the Silver Cup PH. G.R.136,138

1 From the car park, walk (SE) across Harpenden Common following the white post waymarks. Cross Walkers Road (S) and continue on a track through the wood. At the junction with Cravells Road turn L (NE), go down hill under the railway bridge to a road junction. Here turn R (E) into Grove Road and walk along, then first L (N) into Dark Lane passing a school (R). At a row of concrete bollards turn R and immediately L on a path (N). Continue forward (N) with housing L to a road junction, where turn R to a mini roundabout. Cross and continue (N) into a lane with housing L and Aldwickbury Park Golf Club R. Continue (N) along the lane downhill to the sewage plant.

2 Walk under the disused railway bridge, turn L along Marquis Lane to The Marquis of Granby PH. At the PH turn R (NE) and shortly L (NW) into a path alongside the River Lea R. Continue with park L and river R, noting the picturesque weir R. You can cross the river to view the weir, then cross back at the far end of the path (NW). Continue alongside a narrow section of the river R. Go through a gate into the car park at All Saints Church. Cross the front of the church into Station Road, and at the junction keep forward L into Coldharbour Lane. Within a few metres enter a metalled path L, then immediately R onto the old railway path (NW) running parallel to Coldharbour Lane.

3 On reaching the main road look R to notice The Red Cow PH, but turn L (SW) up Westfield Road. Pass Harpenden Cemetery R, and continue alongside railway R.

4 At Hollybush Lane turn R, cross the railway bridge and immediately turn R onto a path, which descends a deep stairway to the commencement of the 'Nicky Line' (SW). This is the route of the former rail link between the main line and Hemel Hempstead.

5 In about 0.5km this path crosses over the A1081, the St Albans/Luton road; continue (SW). After going over a raised crossing path, notice the remains of a railway halt platform with a signal arm R. Pass school R and garden nursery L. Keep forward at the first crossing path, but at the second turn R (W).

6 In a few metres go through a waymarked gap in the corner of hedges. Continue (W) with trees L and golf course R. Just before the end of the wooded area, turn L (S) into it by a waymark post, and follow a clear path with golf course R. At a waymarked gate pass through and turn R (W) into a fenced paddock, alongside the golf course boundary R. Continue down hill through two more gates, turn R onto track (SW) into an open area surrounded by farm buildings. (Note the ancient, but now refurbished barn L at Harpendenbury Farm).

Redbournbury Mill

7 Keep straight on and cross steel footbridge opposite (S) onto the golf course, bear L (S) with grass mound L. Keep to the L edge of the golf course, which is marked by waymark posts. Go through a gate into a meadow, keep forward (SW) to a signposted gate at the Redbourn by-pass. Go through this and the gate opposite, and keep forward (SW) along a wide grassy strip. The way bends L (S). Continue onto a gated track to reach Harpenden Lane.

8 Cross this road and turn L (E) towards the roundabout along the roadside path. At the roundabout, turn R (S) onto the 'Nicky Line' as it runs parallel with the by-pass (A5183). Go past the entrance to the travellers site R. On approaching the bridge over the High Street, Redbourn, the walk continues forward (SW) over it.

Alternatively : If you wish to visit the pleasant village of Redbourn, do not cross the bridge, but turn R and descend the steps to the road. Turn R (NW) to the village, where there are refreshments. Toilets are available at the village hall car park. To continue the walk, return to the bridge, go up the steps and continue forward (SW) over the High Street.

9 In 250m where a path enters from housing R, turn immediately L by a low level transformer onto a grassy track. On reaching the by-pass, cross, then bear R and enter a metalled lane over a stream. The metalled track gives way to a farm track, then a field path, hedge L. Ignore gaps L, with Doolittle Mill now visible ahead. Take narrow path L of the hedge down the side of a fenced field to the Mill. Go through two gates at Dolittle Mill onto Watling Street (A5183), an old Roman road.

10 Cross this road and go through the gate opposite, still following the 'Ver Valley Walk' signs. Continue through two gates and enter a hedged grassy track alongside Redbournbury Mill L. On reaching the farm road, turn L (E) in front of the mill, continue (NE) over two footbridges past Redbournbury Farm R. Where the road bends R, turn L (NW) onto a wide track and in 500m turn R (NE) onto a rising track. In 400m by an oak tree and waymark, bear R (E) across a field, then go through a waymarked gap in the hedge.

11 Continue forward (E) and at the top of the slope, keep forward by a waymark, past a power post R and housing L. Ignore the parallel roadway L, continue on a path between fences. At the far end cross the road into Hawsley Road, continue ahead into Collens Road. Go through a gate in a hedge R and continue to the main road (A1081). A bollard just S of the junction provides a safe crossing on this very busy road. **Alternatively :** You may prefer to use the pleasant Beesonend Lane from Item 11 to Cross Lane, Item 12, see map.

12 Turn R into Cross Lane and in a few metres, turn L onto the golf course (N). Continue parallel with the St Albans Road, but 15m from it, following the white waymark posts back to the car park.

Redbournbury Farm

WALK 15

Devil's Dyke, Wheathampstead

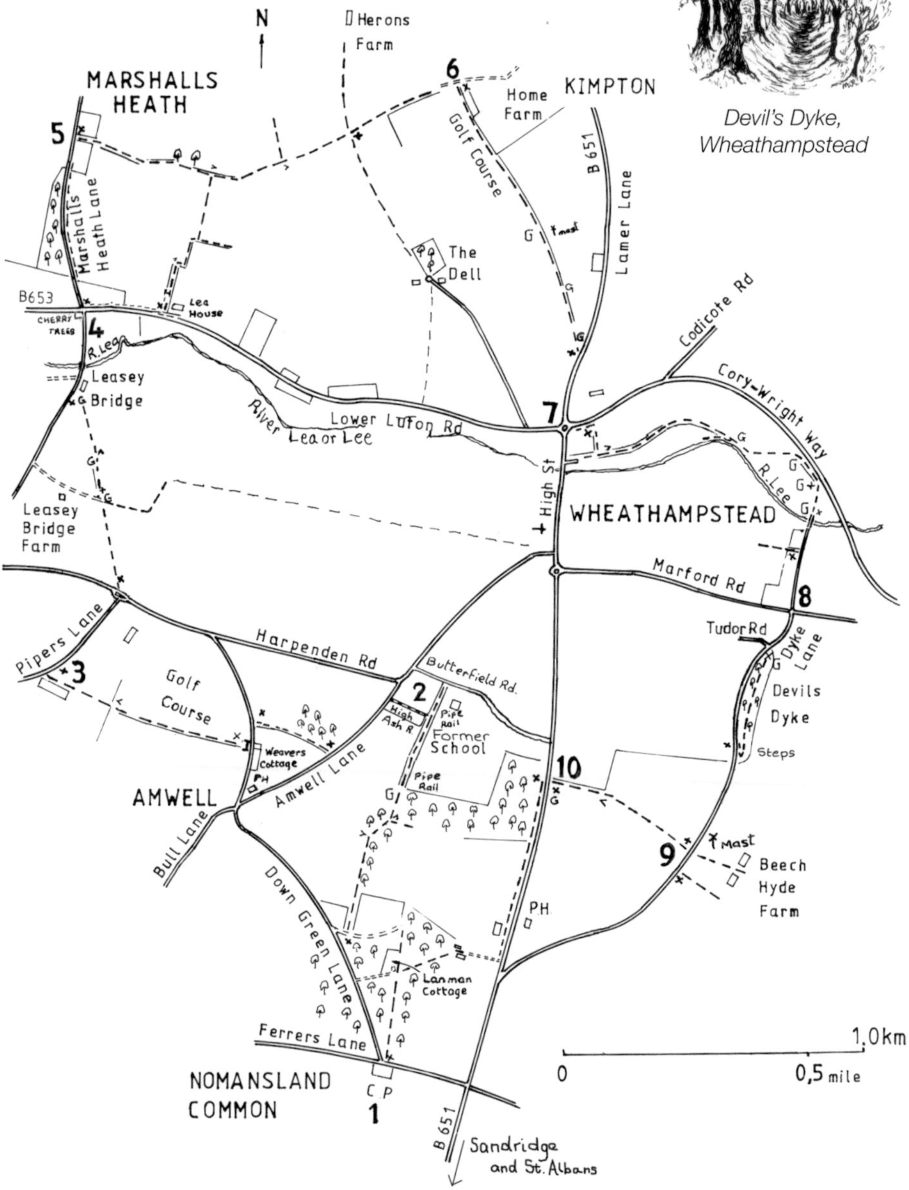

Total Distance 7.0 miles (11.3 km)

CIRCULAR WALK AROUND WHEATHAMPSTEAD

WALK 15

Park in car park on Nomansland Common, opposite junction of Down Green Lane and Ferrers Lane. G.R.172,123

1 Cross the road (N) and go up Down Green Lane. After about 300m, take the second lane R, turn immediately L at a signpost along a path (N) between fences. In about 300m at a waymark sign, turn R (NE) into woodland. Ignore a path R, continue (NE) to a pipe-rail barrier. Follow former school boundary fence (NE).

2 At the housing, take the first path L through a pipe rail barrier into High Ash Road. Go (NW) along this path to its junction with Amwell Lane, along which turn L (SW). In about 250m at a signpost, take the path R (W) to Down Green Lane. Turn L (S) and in about 150m at a signpost opposite 'Weavers Cottage' take the path R (W) along the boundary of the golf course and fields to Pipers Lane.

3 Turn R along this lane (NE) to meet the Harpenden/Wheathampstead road. Cross and at signpost take the path opposite (N), which joins a track near Leasey Bridge Farm. Cross the crossing track to a gate, and follow the swan waymark (N) with hedge L. Continue diagonally across a field to a bungalow called 'Little Croft' into Leasey Bridge Lane. Turn R along this lane, cross the river pausing to admire the picturesque setting. Continue to the Lower Luton Road by the former Cherry Tree PH.

4 Cross the road and continue up Marshalls Heath Lane (N). After about 100m take the path on R in the woods parallel to this road. Continue a further 500m (N) to a bridleway signpost R.

Alternatively : At Item 4, cross the road and turn R along the Lower Luton Road (E). In 600m, just before 'Lee House', is a signpost. Turn L (N) and follow a fenced path. After a short R and L is a waymark post. Continue (N) on a field path. This meets the bridleway from Item 5 where turn R to Item 6.

5 Turn R (E) between houses and continue (NE) across open fields. This clear track continues to a four-way signpost just (S) of Herons Farm. Cross and continue (E) along a path with hedge and golf course R.

6 Cross the track which enters the golf course, turn R at the signpost (SE), follow a hedge then a fence L, down to another gate. Continue (SE) through a gate to a further gate to the Kimpton/Wheathampstead road (B651). Cross the road, turn R (S) and go down to the roundabout.

7 Cross at the traffic island and turn L along the Cory-Wright Way (E). In about 60m turn R (S) at the bridleway sign, passing Abbott John Mews R. In a further 30m turn L (E) along a concrete surfaced bridleway. This soon becomes a path through trees giving views of the River Lea R. After passing through two gates, the path continues between fences on each side alongside the main road. It then meets a gravel lane, crosses the River Lea and continues (S) as Sheepcote Lane to the Marford Road.

8 Cross this road, continue (S) up Dyke Lane. In 70m, near the junction with Tudor Road at a footpath sign L, enter a gate into Devil's Dyke. (Note the display board giving historical details). Continue (S) and at the far end follow the sharp loop R (N) up steps. In 20m turn L out to the lane. Turn L (S) and in 100m is Beech Hyde Farm.

9 Turn R at the signpost opposite the farm entrance, take the clear path across a field (NW). Continue with housing fence R to the Sandridge/Wheathampstead road (B651).

10 Cross the road and take the path L (S) parallel with the road to Nomansland Common. Turn R along a gravel track (W) behind the pavilion, then bear L along a grassy path through the woods (SW). At 'Lanman Cottage' continue (S) through the wood to the car park.

WALK 16

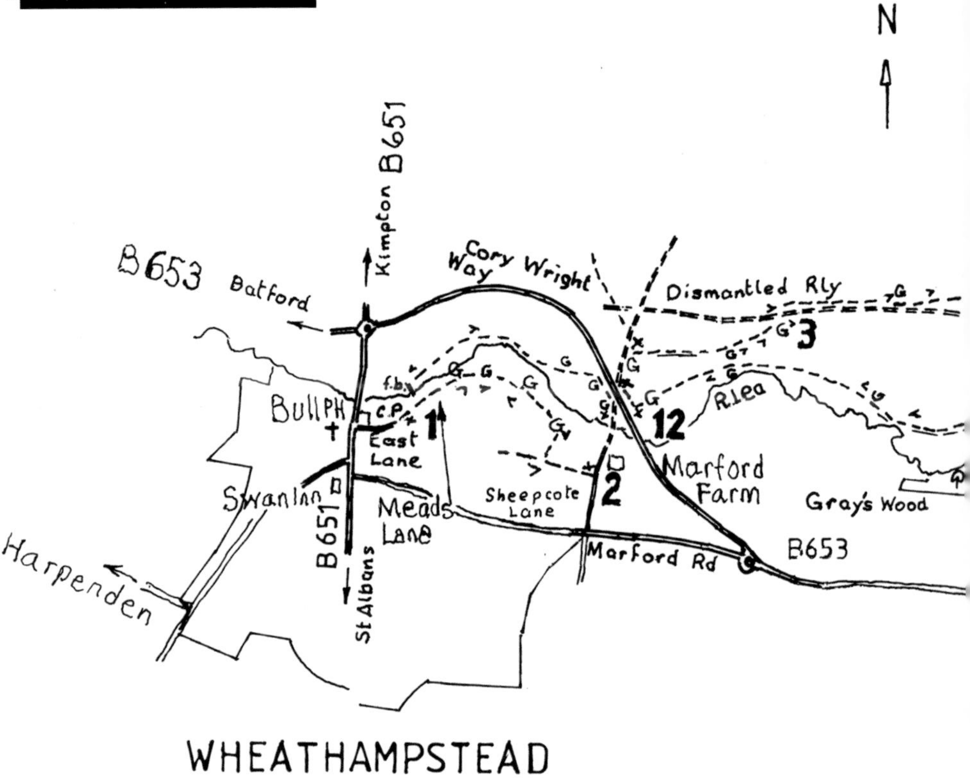

Ayot Green

Total Distance 9.0 miles (14.5 km)
Shorter route 7.3 miles (11.7 km)

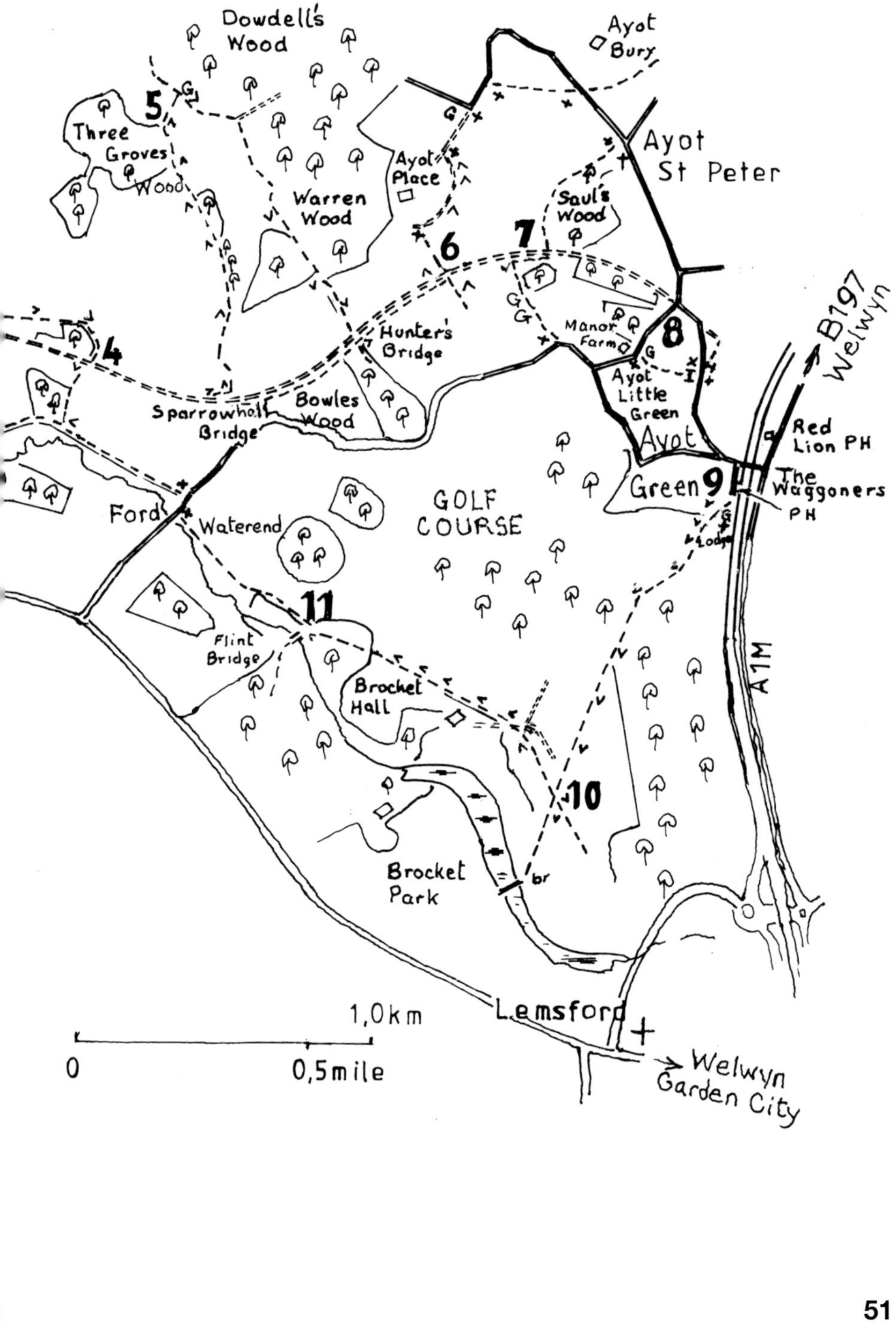

Dowdell's Wood
Ayot Bury
5
Three Groves Wood
Ayot Place
Warren Wood
Ayot St Peter
Saul's Wood
6
7
4
Hunter's Bridge
Manor Farm
8
Ayot Little Green
B197 Welwyn
Sparrowhall Bridge
Bowles Wood
Ayot Green
9
Red Lion PH
The Waggoners PH
Ford
Waterend
GOLF COURSE
Lodge
11
Flint Bridge
Brocket Hall
A1M
10
Brocket Park
br
Lemsford
1,0km
0
0,5mile
Welwyn Garden City

WHEATHAMPSTEAD, AYOT ST PETER, BROCKET PARK

WALK 16

Park in public car park in East Lane, (beyond The Bull car park), Wheathampstead. G.R.178,141

1 From the car park, turn L into East Lane (NE), bear L into Meads Lane, which soon becomes an asphalt track. Go through barrier to a 4-way signpost, follow the sign 'Sheepcote Lane l/2m' ahead (E) with hedge R. Where the hedge bends R, continue ahead (SE) into a fenced path with paddock L. Go through kissing gate, continue (SE) through three more gates, turning R (SW) onto a fenced path to a waymarked T-junction of paths. Turn L (E) with fence L and allotments R, and go between posts into a narrow path between houses into Sheepcote Lane.

2 Turn L (N) along this lane past Marford Farm R, cross the River Lea and continue under Cory-Wright Way. In about 100m by an iron gate, turn R in front of it through a gap by another iron gate into a field path with hedge R. Continue (E), ignoring the gate R, to a fence gap, where the path bears L (NE) with fence R, to a gate in the far corner. Go through this gate, down the slope to the dismantled railway track called 'Ayot Green Way'.

3 Cross this track, bear L for a few metres to a bridleway sign opposite, where turn R (E) along a fenced path which climbs alongside the track (R). This path descends (E) into a valley, through a gate at a wood corner R. Go uphill to a waymarked post and across a field (E) to another waymark, into a further field with edge of wood R. Turn R (S) round the boundary of this wood to rejoin the track.

4 Turn L (E) along the track for 500m to a waymarked path by a seat L. Take this path (E) up to a wide gravel crossing track at a bridge. Turn L (N) on this track uphill past a corner of a wood R. Note the wide views (S). Continue onto a path (N) following a line of oaks past a small wood R. Continue (N) across a field towards a wood corner L, then follow the edge of this wood L. The path turns R (NE) with hedge L to meet a bridleway at a T-junction by a double gate.

5 Turn R (SE) along this bridleway with the edge of the wood L. After 600m the footpath enters the wood for 150m. On emerging from the wood, go ahead to a gap L in the hedge and continue (SE) along a field edge with hedge R. Ignore the steps R, go under the railway bridge (called Hunters Bridge), and immediately turn L (NE) following the foot of the railway embankment L. In 350m turn L (NW) through a gap near a power line junction. Cross the railway track to a gap opposite near a power post, onto a field path (NW).

6 Cross the field to meet a narrow service road at a bend, turn R (E) at the signpost. Follow this road past rhododendrons to a T-junction and turn R (NE). Leave this drive road through the gateway doors with lodge R into a road at a bend. Continue along the road (NE) for 100m, turn R to cross a signposted gap in a hedge near a large oak. Cross the field (E) to a signposted gap in the hedge opposite out to a road. Turn R (SE) along the road and just before the road junction turn R (SW) into a signposted path into a wood. Avoid a fork L near a garden gate, continue downhill (SW) with edge of wood R, emerging through a gap in the fence onto the railway track again.

7 Cross the track, then go through gap opposite (S). Turn sharp R (W) and follow path parallel to the old railway track for 100m to a waymark post. Turn L (S) across a field to the wood corner, enter the wood (S) and follow the downhill path with wood L. Near the bottom of the slope go through a kissing gate and follow a fence R (S). Cross this fence at a gate into a hedged uphill path (S). Go between posts, and turn L (SE) at the road passing Manor Farm Cottage L. At the T-junction turn L to Ayot Little Green. A few metres past Manor Farm L bear R (E) across the green past the waymarked chestnut tree L.

8 Cross the drive in front of a house R into a narrow path with a gate marked 'No bridleway'. Go through into a field, bear R (E) to follow the hedge R down to a stile at the road. Turn R (S) along the road to Ayot Green, bear L (SE) past attractive cottages to a bridge over the A1(M). Here a detour to the Red Lion PH may be made by crossing the bridge and turning L for 150m.

9 Immediately before crossing the bridge, turn R (S) into Brickwall Close, once part of the old Great North Road. Just past The Waggoners L, go through a kissing gate R (SW) onto a fenced path. Go through a fence gap (SW) into Brocket Park with lodge L. Follow the waymarks through conifers, cross the golf course, avoiding paths which fork L or R, continue (SW) up a slope onto the large golf course. Take the waymarked path ahead (SW) across the course, heading for the edge of woodland.

10 At the estate road, cross and turn sharp R (NW) onto a fenced path with woodland L. Cross the estate road, turn L downhill with fence L. Continue uphill (NW) with views of Brocket Hall and the lake (S). This well waymarked path leads to gap in a wood boundary ahead. Go through the wood (NW) along an embankment with fence L, then descend steeply to a crossing track. (A short detour L leads to a flint bridge over the River Lea in pleasant woodland surroundings).

11 Cross the track, continue (NW) along a path, first with fence L, then R. This follows the river L and emerges onto a road at Waterend, with ford L. Turn R, then in a few metres turn L (NW) opposite the large Jacobean house. This gravel bridleway follows the river with hedge L. In 500m at a bend, continue ahead (W) along path through wood R. Go through a kissing gate into water meadows (W). Continue through a gate to a signposted gate by Cory-Wright Way. Turn R.

12 Turn L down steps and go under the bridge. In 50m turn sharp R (NW) at a gate onto a fenced path to another gate. Continue (W) through a wooden gate, then bear L into a hedge gap to a permissive path following the river L. Cross the footbridge L and retrace the outward route along Meads Lane and East Lane to the car park.

Alternatively : This walk can be shortened by keeping on the old railway track from Item 3 to Item 7, but the walk as described is more pleasant.

Brocket Hall

WALK 17

Stapleford Church

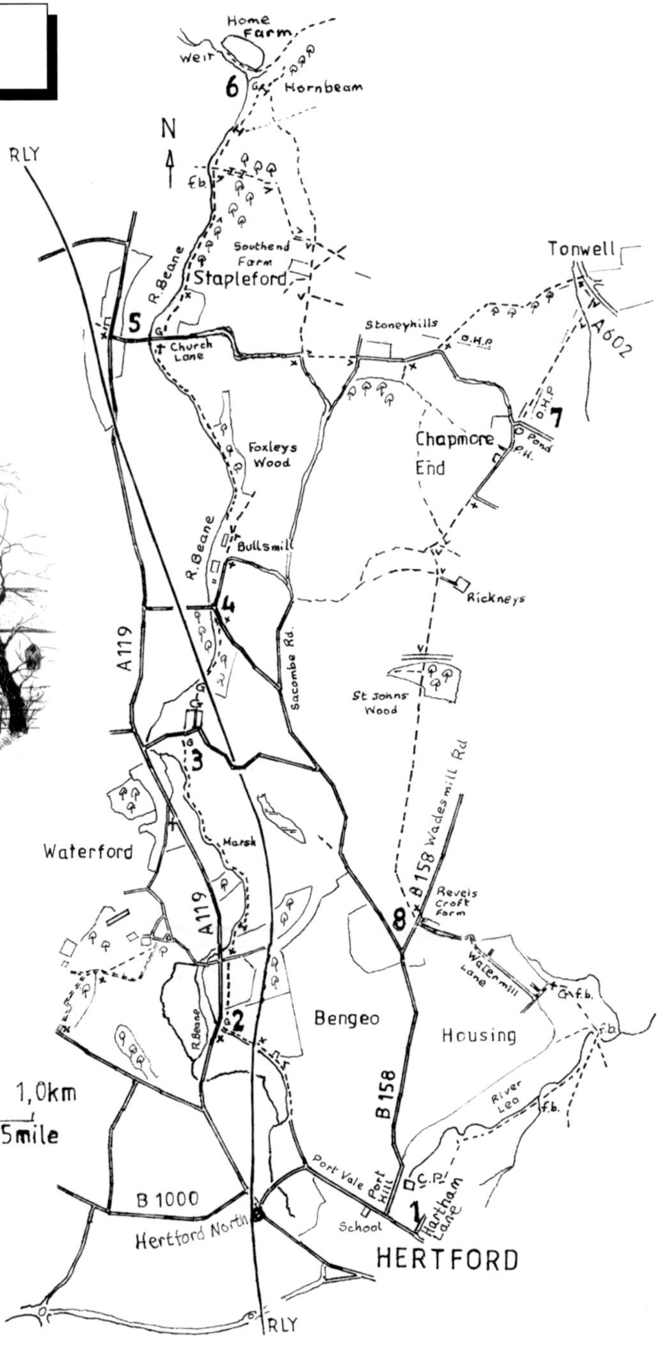

Total Distance 9.4 miles (15.2 km)

HERTFORD, WATERFORD, STAPLEFORD, TONWELL, CHAPMORE END

WALK 17

Park in public car park (charge) in Hartham Lane, off Cowbridge, Hertford. G.R.324,130

1 Leave the car park by the exit road, cross bridge over the River Beane into Port Hill (B158). Turn L (S) downhill and at T-junction at the foot of the hill, turn R into Port Vale. Follow this road (NW) past Mill Mead School to the end of the housing. Continue ahead (N) along a pleasant track through woodland, which follows the river L to the old Molewood Pumping Station. Continue (NW) along the bank of the river R, go under a railway bridge to the main Hertford/Stevenage road (A119), at a gate.

2 Turn R (N) along the pavement for about 400m until opposite the entrance to Goldings. Take the path R that leads down to the river at Waterford Marshes. Follow this path (N) along the river L. Note the village of Waterford with its church spire L. Continue by the river to the houses ahead and emerge through a kissing gate onto a road.

3 Turn R (E) along the road and in about 50m turn L at the signpost into Barleycroft. Go through the housing (N) to a metal gate by the last house, No.21. Go through the gate and walk ahead (N) to a kissing gate. Go under the railway bridge and follow the river again. Continue (N) to a road junction.

4 Here turn L and within 50m turn R onto road, which leads towards a metal farm gate. Ignoring the narrow lane R, go through the gate. Pass large blockwork barn L and take waymarked path L, which meets the river again. This pleasant path follows the river for about 1km to Stapleford Church R.

5 Turn R (E) for about 50m then L (N) into Clusterbolts Road. Continue along and into the wood following the river L. Continue with field fence R and river hedge L, past a footbridge L. In a further 200m at an estate boundary cross a ladder stile. In a further 400m the river widens and divides just (S) of Home Farm.

6 Note a kissing gate R leading to a wide track which runs (S). Take this track (S) and in about 900m go past Southend Farm R. Continue to a sharp bend in Church Lane. Here turn L (E) along 'Herts Way' footpath. Go through the hedge gap into Stony Hills Road and continue (E) along the road towards Chapmore End. Where the road turns sharp R under electric power lines, bear L. The path continues (NE) over an open field, then with hedge R to Ware Road (A602). Turn R (SE) at the bottom of the wooden steps leading up to the A602 and continue for about 100m with hedge L and fence R to a second set of wooden steps. Here turn R (SW) at next stile, go downhill over a footbridge and continue straight on uphill, with hedge R, to road at Chapmore End.

7 Turn R, then L round pond, past The Woodman PH. Keep on the road (SW) and where it turns sharp L, continue ahead (SW) along a bridleway to an open field R, with waymark L. Continue keeping hedge L until a three-way crossing, with farm L. Keep straight on over concrete road through St John's Wood, then straight ahead across open fields (S) to Wadesmill Road (B158).

8 Cross this into Watermill Lane North and continue (SE) to the bottom. Bear L (E) onto a bridleway, follow path round to the R with wood R and house fences L. At the end of gravel path, continue along road with houses L to a T-junction. Here turn L downhill, bear R (SE) to bridge over the river. Before bridge, turn R. Go through a gate, then straight ahead with hedge R over metal footbridge. Go straight on to cross a gated bridge over River Lea. Turn R and follow path (SW) along river bank and go over a wooden bridge. With weir L, continue along bank of river R to tennis courts, then turn L across common to car park.

WALK 18

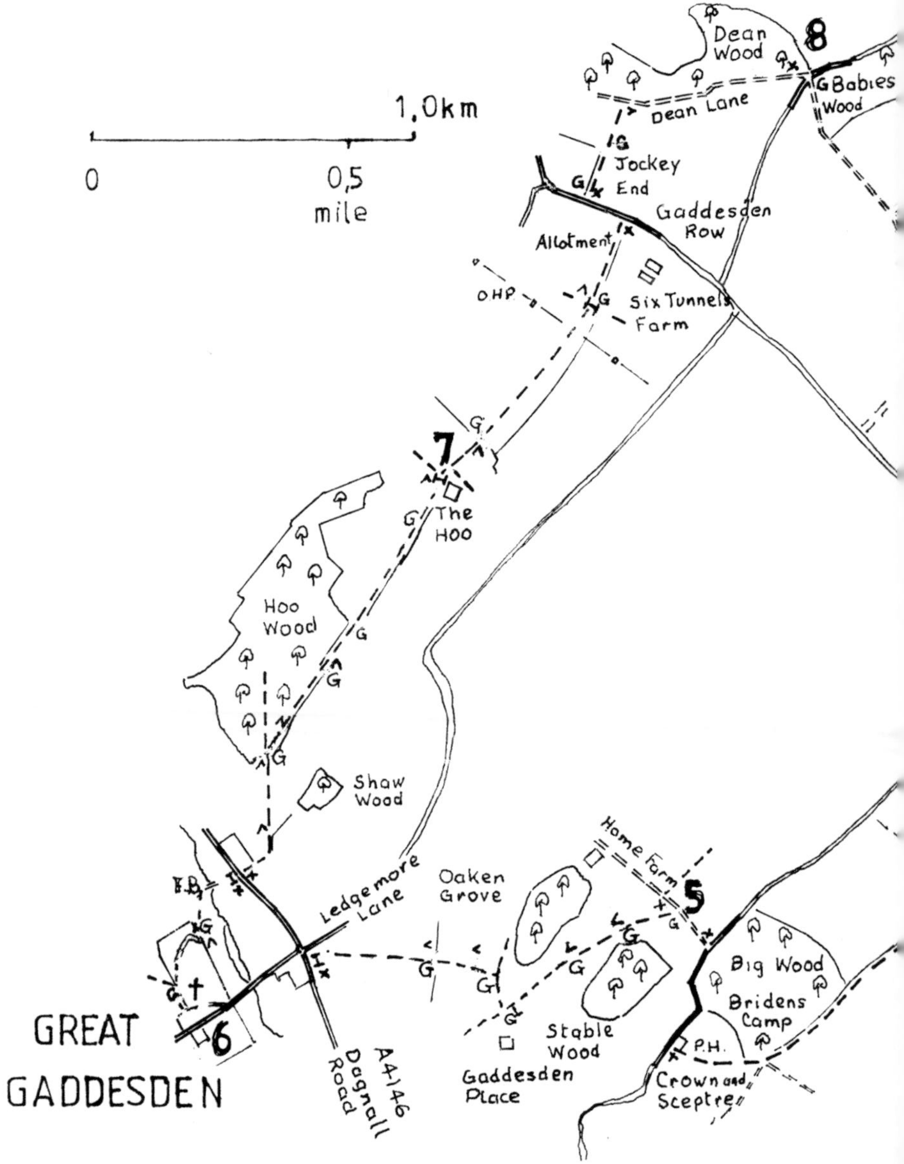

Total Distance 10.8 miles (17.4 km)

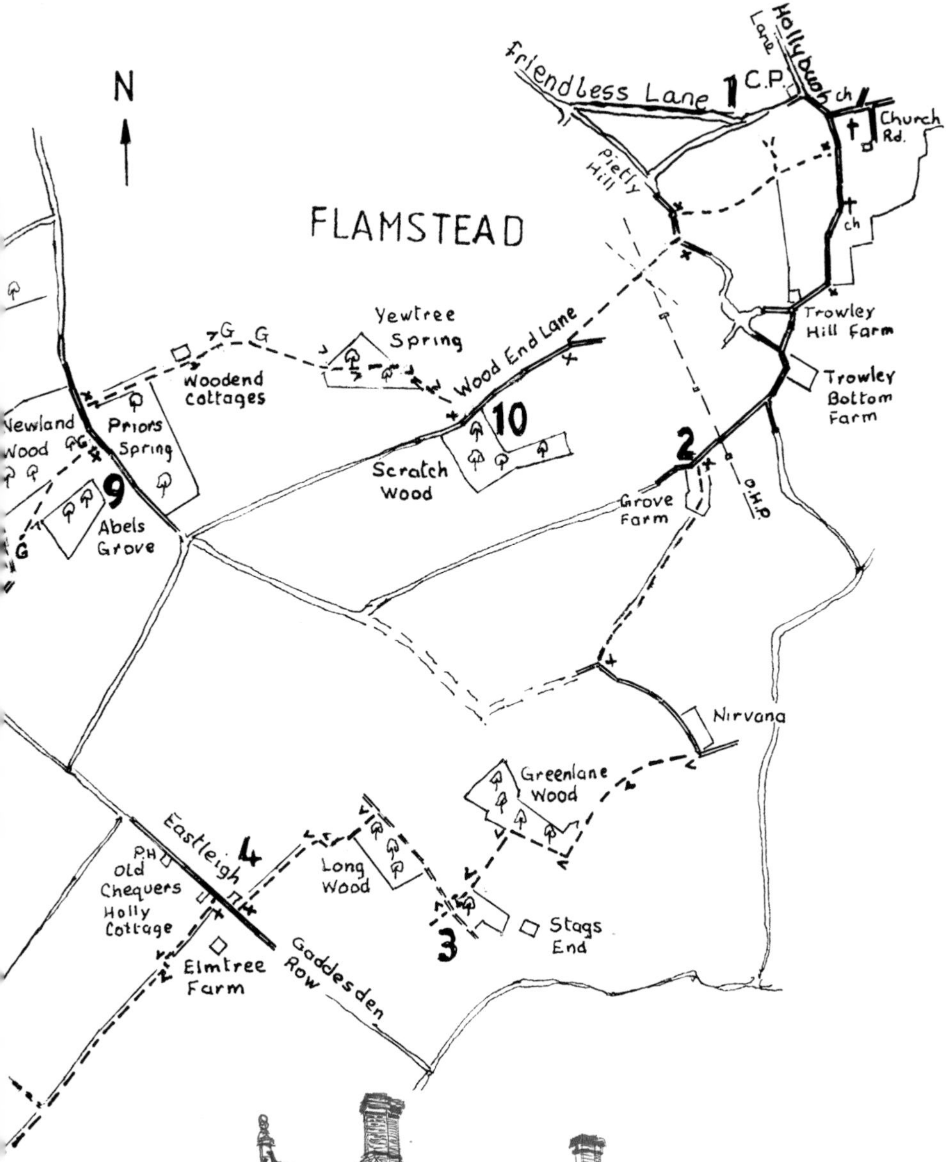

The Saunders Almshouses, Flamstead

FLAMSTEAD, GREAT GADDESDEN, JOCKEY END

WALK 18

Park in Flamstead recreation ground car park at the junction of Friendless Lane and Hollybush Lane. G.R.077,147

1 From the car park turn R (SE). Continue (S) past the church L into Trowley Hill Road. At Trowley Hill Farm R, turn L down White Hill (S). Pass Trowley Bottom Farm L and take the R fork uphill (SW) to Grove Farm L. Enter the farmyard (S) and walk between buildings keeping to the gravel track, which goes between a barn L and the main farm buildings R.

2 Continue (SW) up a well-defined track with hedge R to a crossing drovers way. Turn L (SE) along this crushed concrete track. Where this track turns sharp L just before 'Nirvana' L, turn R (SW) through a hedge gap into a field. Cross this to the SE corner of Greenlane Wood. Turn R (NW) along the edge of this wood R for 250m to a waymark. Turn L (SW) across the field to the W side of the wood on the skyline, to a track. Continue (SW) with wood L to a crossing bridleway.

3 Turn R (NW) along this with Longwood L. In 400m at the corner of the wood turn L (SW), with the edge of the wood L and field R. Turn R (NW) (signpost to Bridens Camp) and in a few metres L (SW) with hedge R out to Gaddesden Row alongside 'Eastleigh'.

4 Turn R (NW) along this road and in 75m turn L (SW) onto a path alongside 'Holly Cottage' R. Continue (SW) with hedge L, and in 150m at a hedge gap, go through and continue on a gravel track (SW) with hedge R. This track leads to Bridens Camp R then bends (W) to the Crown and Sceptre PH. Turn R (NE) along the road, taking great care round the S-bends. Turn L along Home Farm Lane.

5 After 75m, go through a gate L into a field. Continue (SW) through two more gates, heading for another gate just to the R of Gaddesden Place. Do not go through this gate, but turn R (N) with fence L to another gate in 100m. Bear L and continue (W) downhill through a gate and into an open field. Continue diagonally across to a signposted gate in Dagnall Road (A4146) at it's junction with Ledgemore Lane. Cross the road with care and enter Great Gaddesden village.

6 Walk up the short lane (W), Church Meadow, through the lych gate into the churchyard. Pass the church R and cross a stile in the top L corner of the churchyard wall. Turn sharp R (N) and follow churchyard wall to two adjoining gates. Turn R into a housing estate, passing a row of garages L. At a sharp bend in the road, continue (N) through a gate to the flood plain of the River Gade. Cross the footbridge (NE) to a stile on the A4146. Cross this road to a track beside a row of houses L. Follow the hedge R to a hedge corner, then take the path due N through a gate into Hoo Wood. Immediately on entering the wood, turn R (NE) to follow inside the wood boundary R. Go through a gate onto a headland path (NE), now outside the wood boundary L. Go through a gate into a meadow with fence R, cross a stile, passing The Hoo house R.

7 Go through hedge gap, across a field (NE) through a gate into a wide meadow. Continue (NE) parallel to the hedge R, but about 50m from it. After going under power lines, cross a stile into an allotment area L. This track leads to a signpost in Gaddesden Row. Turn L (NW) for 150m towards Jockey End to a row of houses R. Turn R (NE) at the signpost before the end of these houses, pass the small play area, and go through a gate onto a path L. This leads down to a gap in the hedge in Dean Lane. Turn R (E) along this pleasant lane for about 700m to a road.

8 Cross the road to a track (S) into Babies Wood, which may be muddy. Continue (SE) along the edge of Newland's Wood. In 75m beyond the far corner of the wood, turn sharp L (NE) through a gate into a field between Newland's Wood L and Abel's Grove R. Continue to the signposted gate at the (NE) corner of the wood to a road.

9 Turn L and in 50m turn R (NE) along a lane to Little Woodend Cottages L. Continue (E), then just past the cottages between sheds L and fence R, go through a gate R and take the field edge path (E) to another gate, then bear R (SE) towards Yewtree Spring Wood. Go through a gap into this wood and another at the far edge of the wood. Turn R (SE) and follow the edge of the wood R. Continue (SE) across an open field through a gap into Wood End Lane.

10 Turn L (NE) and in 360m at a bend in the road, fork L (NE) into a field down to the bottom of the valley. Continue (NE) under the power lines, then uphill to a stile at Pietly Hill. Turn L along the road, and in 100m turn R into a field. Continue (NE) towards Flamstead Church; at Trowley Hill Road turn L and back to the car park.

Great Gaddesden Church

WALK 19

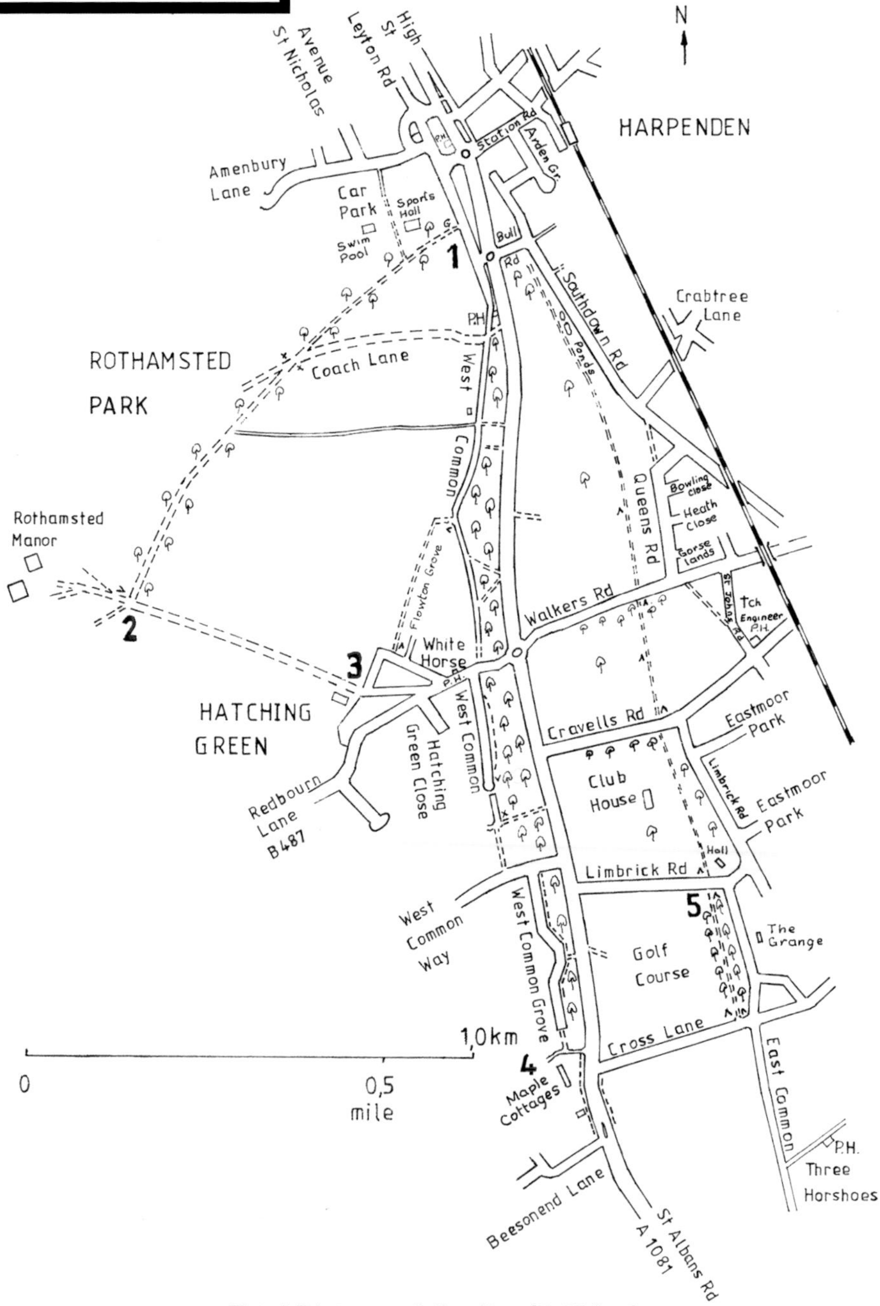

N
HARPENDEN
High St
Leyton Rd
St Nicholas Avenue
Station Rd
Arden Gr
P.H.
Amenbury Lane
Car Park
Sports Hall
Swim Pool
G
Bull
1
Rd
Southdown Rd
Ponds
Crabtree Lane
P.H.
ROTHAMSTED PARK
Coach Lane
West Common
Queens Rd
Bowling Close
Heath Close
Gorse lands
Rothamsted Manor
2
Flowton Grove
Walkers Rd
St Johns Rd
Tch Engineer P.H.
3
White Horse P.H.
HATCHING GREEN
West Common
Hatching Green Close
Cravells Rd
Eastmoor Park
Limbrick Rd
Eastmoor Park
Club House
Redbourn Lane B487
Limbrick Rd
Hall
West Common Way
West Common Grove
5
The Grange
Golf Course
Cross Lane
1,0km
0
0,5
mile
4
Maple Cottages
East Common
P.H.
Three Horshoes
Beesonend Lane
St Albans Rd A 1081

Total Distance 3.5 miles (5.63 km)

ROTHAMSTED PARK, HARPENDEN COMMON

WALK 19

A short walk suitable for families with push chairs.

By bus : Alight at The George PH at the southern end of the High Street, Harpenden, bear R into Leyton Road, continue south to the entrance of Rothamsted Park.

By train : Turn L down Station Road to the High Street, then cross and bear L into Leyton Road to the entrance of Rothamsted Park.

By car : Park in Amenbury Lane car park, go south into Rothamsted Park past the Sports Hall L. Turn R along the avenue of trees.

1 Enter Rothamsted Park by the brick gate posts, opposite the town sign on the green. Continue (SW) through the avenue of lime trees ignoring the fork in the track.

2 At the T-junction with another avenue, note the outbuildings of Rothamsted Manor R. Turn L (SE) along this avenue to the entrance and emerge onto Hatching Green

3 Continue L then R round the green, passing The White Horse Inn, L into Redbourn Lane. Turn L and in a few metres R (S) into West Common where there is a path through the trees parallel to the road. At West Common Way turn L and almost at once R (S) into West Common Grove. Keep to the L side of this road, noting a pleasant path just inside the tree line.

4 At the end of the carriageway, a path continues (S) through the trees to a crossing lane at Maple Cottages. Turn L (E) to the main St Albans road (A1081). Turn R (S) along this to a bollard island where it is safe to cross this busy road. Retrace your steps (N) on the other side, then turn R (E) into Cross Lane. Continue (E) then just before reaching East Common, turn L (N) along a bridle path between an avenue of trees.

5 Cross Limbrick Road and continue (N) on a path along the edge of the golf course, parallel with the bridleway (N). Cross Cravells Road (N) then Walkers Road (N). At two crossing tracks, keep R to a cinder track with ponds R. Keep parallel with the line of ponds to Bull Road back to the starting point L.

Alternatively : In wet weather at Item 5 facing Limbrick Hall, turn R and then L along Limbrick Road. At the junction with Cravells Road turn R (E) by the post box. At The Engineer PH, turn L (N) into St John's Road, then opposite the vicarage, fork L onto a path to Walkers Road. Cross into Queen's Road, and where this turns R, keep ahead (N) on a path to Southdown Road. Continue (N) using the pavement on the opposite side passing three ponds L. Turn L into Bull Road back to the starting point.

Leyton Road, Harpenden

WALK 20

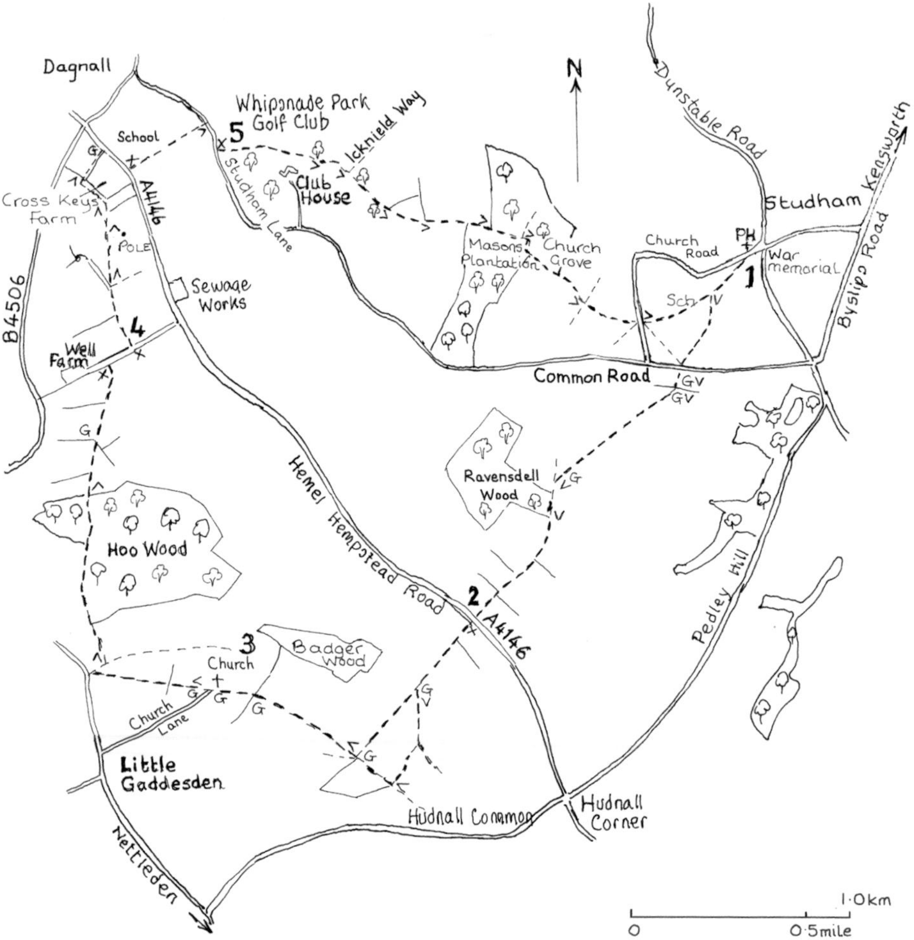

Total Distance 6.7 miles (10.72 km)

THREE COUNTIES WALK:

STUDHAM, LITTLE GADDESDEN, DAGNALL

WALK 20

Park along Church Road, Studham. G.R.023,158

Alternatively : This walk can also be started from Little Gaddesden Church (Item 3). G.R.997,138. Park outside the church, or next to the Bowls Club in Church Lane.

1 Follow Church Road for 100m, then bear L (SW) on bridleway across the common to the junction of paths adjacent to a house called 'The Old School'. Bear L (S) onto a footpath up a slope. Cross Common Road, continuing through a gate opposite, and after 100m go through another gate. Bear R (SW), following part of the Chiltern Way across a field and through a gate in a hedge towards Ravensdell Wood. Go through a gate in the hedge and turn L (S) onto a bridleway, continuing with wood R, then hedge R (SW) to the Hemel Hempstead Road (A4146).

2 Cross road and continue on path with hedge L for about 400m, then turn L (S) through a gate and follow path along the side of hill, with trees R. Pass some houses R and meet an access road, then turn sharp R (NW) onto the access road for 30m. Turn L onto a signposted path between houses and through two gates. Continue (NW) along headland hedge R, through two more gates to Little Gaddesden Church R.

3 Take the fenced path (W) along the north side of the church car park, across three fields and several gates almost to Nettleden Road. Do not go through the gate into Nettleden Road, but turn sharp R, then immediately L onto a new path (E) for about 50m. Here turn L (N) along a bridleway, passing gardens L and enter Hoo Wood. Continue through the wood for about 550m. On leaving the wood, cross two fields with gates, and head slightly R towards a hedge, continuing (N) with hedge L to join a farm track. Here turn R for 100m.

4 Turn L and continue (N) with hedge L, then cross an open field to a hedge corner.

Alternative A : Go diagonally across the next field to another hedge corner in line with an electricity pole. Continue with hedge R to farm entrance. DO NOT ENTER. Follow diversion path, keeping hedge R, then sharp R round the outside of Cross Keys Farm to Main Road South (A4146). Turn R along this road until reaching Dagnall village school L.

Alternative B : Turn R onto the bridleway and out to Main Road South (A4146). Turn L (NW) along the road to Dagnall village school L.

To continue, cross the A4146 and go up the path (NE) to Studham Lane. Turn R and after 100m turn L by 'The Bungalow' and up the long steep slope onto the golf course, passing 'Keepers Cottage' L near the top.

5 Continue ahead through a gate (E) keeping the clubhouse R and follow a clearly way-marked path through a line of trees. On leaving the golf course, continue (E) on a path, bear L and continue, keeping hedge to the R, following this into Mason's Plantation. Proceed through Mason's Plantation for about 200m to a right angle bend and turn R. After a further 100m turn L following a path alongside the wood. After approximately 100m, descend through a narrow gap (R) into a field, then through a gate with hedge L, emerging at Valley Road. Cross the road and follow path (E), with hedge L to school, then (NE) along the common to Studham War Memorial and back to the start.

The Red Lion, Studham

WALK 21

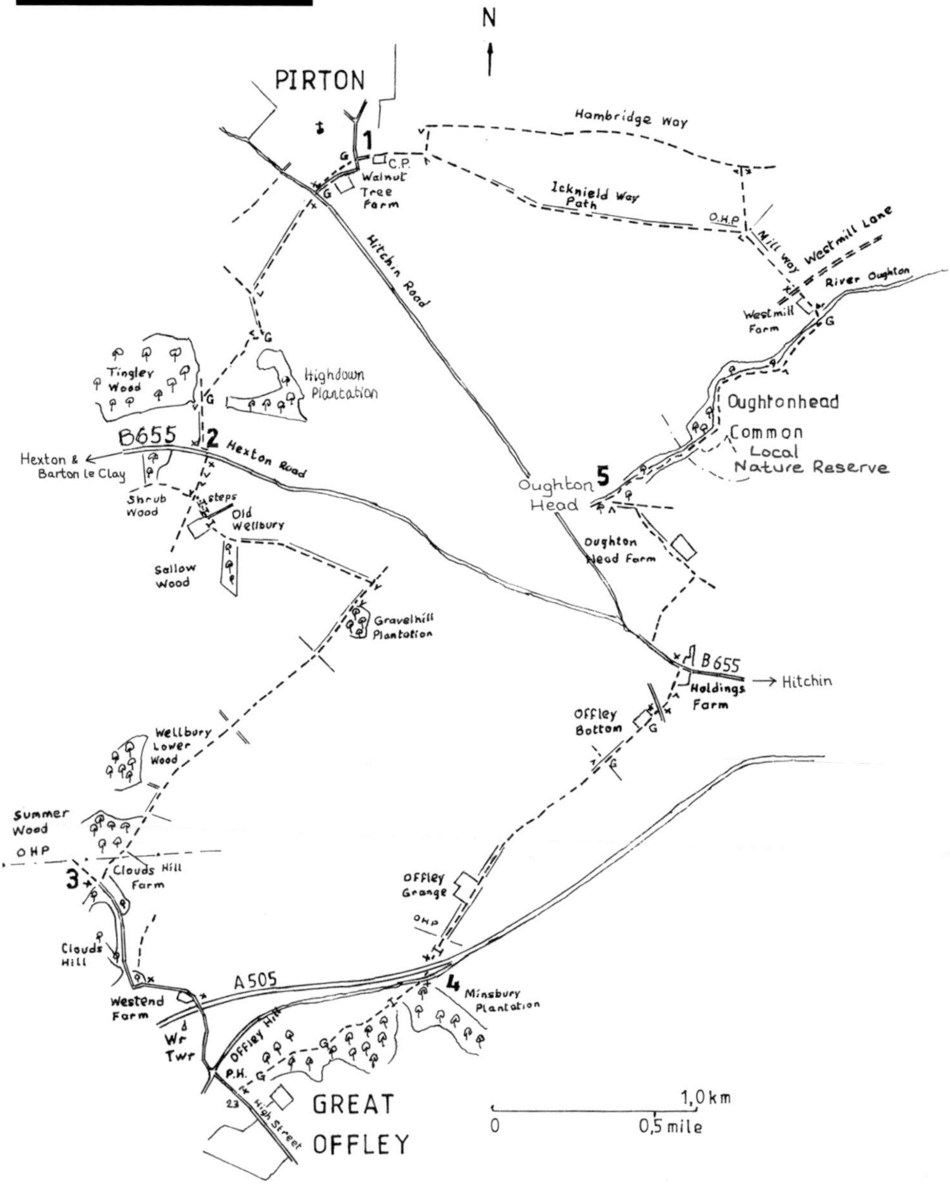
N
PIRTON
1
C.P.
Walnut Tree Farm
Hambridge Way
Icknield Way Path
O.H.P
Mill Way
Westmill Lane
River Oughton
Westmill Farm
Hitchin Road
Tingley Wood
Highdown Plantation
Oughtonhead Common Local Nature Reserve
B655
2
Hexton Road
Hexton & Barton le Clay
Shrub Wood
steps
Old Wellbury
Sallow Wood
5
Oughton Head
Oughton Head Farm
Gravelhill Plantation
B655
Hitchin
Holdings Farm
Offley Bottom
Wellbury Lower Wood
Summer Wood
OHP
3
Clouds Hill Farm
Clouds Hill
Offley Grange
OHP
A505
4
Minsbury Plantation
Westend Farm
Wr Twr
Offley Hill
P.H.
High Street
GREAT OFFLEY
1,0 km
0
0,5 mile

Total Distance 9.2 miles (14.8 km)

PIRTON, OFFLEY, OUGHTONHEAD

WALK 21

Park in Pirton recreation ground car park. GR.150,315

1 On leaving the car park, cross the road and go through a gate to a path (SW) towards the far left corner of the field. Go through a gate in the corner of the field and turn R to a T-junction. Cross to a path (SW) with hedge R to meet a crossing track. Turn L (SE) with hedge R. Bear R (W) through a gate into a field, follow path uphill to a gate in a hedge. Go through, cross a track and continue with hedge R downhill (S). Turn L alongside the Hexton Road (B655) for 50m, then cross the road with care to a path opposite.

2 Continue straight on up a grassy path (SW), turn L at the third waymarked crossing path. Go down steps, over two stiles and cross the access road to Old Wellbury. Bear L and go uphill (SE) along a grassy path to the corner of Sallow Wood. Pass the wood R then go along a hedge L (SE) to a crossing bridleway. Turn R (SW) between hedges, passing Gravelhill Plantation L. Keeping to hedge R, go through a gap in the hedge ahead. Continue (SW) across a large field heading for the power pylon ahead. Ignore a crossing track, go through another hedge gap and continue (SW) uphill with hedge R. Pass Summer Wood R, go under power lines through a hedge gap and emerge onto road junction at Clouds Hill Farm.

3 Turn L (SE) and follow the lane over the A505 into School Lane to the junction with Offley Hill. Cross into the High Street and pass The Green Man PH. In 100m turn L alongside a house, No.23, go through a gate, bear R (NE) towards woodland. Go through another gap and keep parallel with the woodland. In 150m look for a hidden gate R, cross and bear L (NE) downhill through a wood. Emerge from the wood, keeping to the path downhill with fence R. Cross a stile by a large tree stump, then go along a track (NE) to the Offley feeder road.

4 Bear R, cross the road then bear L past cottages R. Go through a hedge gap, cross the A505 with care using the R and L gap in the central reservation. Cross the stile opposite, then follow a grassy track (NE) under power lines past Offley Grange L, then Offley Bottom Farm L. Go through a gate to the road, then after a short R and L, follow the path uphill past Holdings Farm to the B655. Cross the road with care, turn L, then in about 100m turn R (NE) onto a track. On reaching a T-junction turn L (NW). In 100m bear L off the track onto a field edge path with hedge R, past Oughton Head Farm R. At a T-junction turn L (W).

5 In about 150m ignore the track R, but continue into woodland, where bear R (NE) down steps at Oughton Head. Continue (NE) alongside the river L for 1.5km on a pleasant path through the Oughton Head Local Nature Reserve to West Mill Farm L. Go through a gate and cross the bridge (NW) and continue uphill to a T-junction. Here a short R and L leads into Mill Way (NW). Continue on this wide track to the junction of three power lines. Turn L (W) onto the Icknield Way path with hedge R. Ignore a track from the R, go through a gate into the recreation ground and the car park.

Alternatively : In wet weather you can continue N at the power line junction for 200m, then turn L into Hambridge Way. In 1km turn L through a gate, then R at a crossing path into the recreation ground.

Pirton Church

WALK 22

15th Century brass,
St Helen's Church,
Wheathampstead

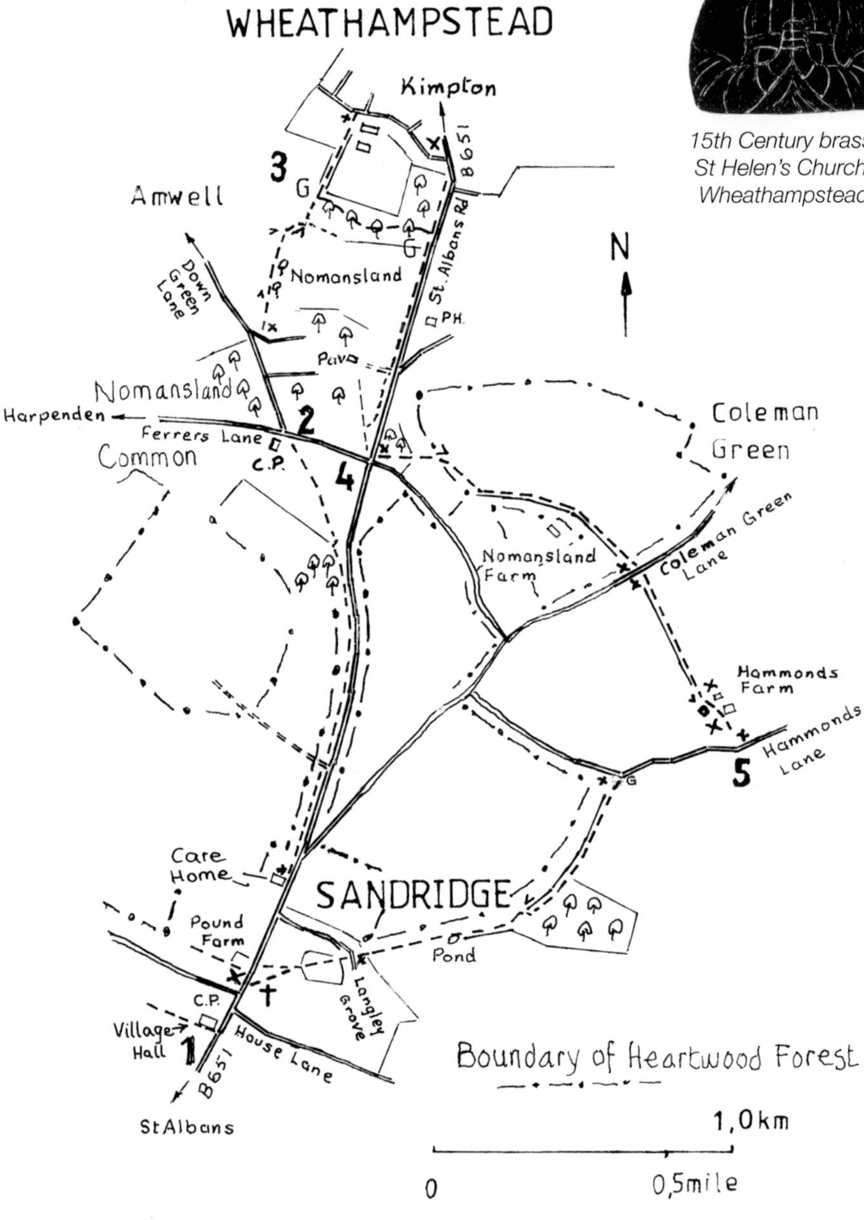

Total Distance 5.3 miles (8.5 km)

SANDRIDGE, WHEATHAMPSTEAD

WALK 22

Park in Sandridge public car park by the village hall. G.R.169,104

1 From the car park, turn L (N) along the High Street (B651). Continue through the village passing the elderly care home L. At the signpost bear L and continue (N) parallel to the road along a field edge with hedge R for 1.5km. Where this hedge turns L, go through it, then down steps and bear diagonally L (NW) across Nomansland Common towards the car park on the Common.

2 Cross Ferrers Lane and go (N) up Down Green Lane opposite for 300m. At the second road junction, turn R and in 10m L (N) at the signpost. Continue (N) past a farmyard R and a copse of conifer trees, then alongside a woodland strip R. Turn R at a waymarked gap, through wood, across the corner of field (NE) to a path junction. Bear L (N) through the wood to a kissing gate R.

3 Go through the gate. (This is a permissive path). In a few metres bear R and follow a grassy path (E) through the nature reserve to exit via a gate at the St Albans road (B651). Turn R (S) along a downhill path with road and hedge L, out to the cricket ground on Nomansland Common.

4 Bear L (S) towards the cross-roads. Here turn L (E) to cross the St Albans road and follow the bridleway sign. Continue (E) along this path bearing slightly R. Continue (E) then (SE) with hedge R to Coleman Green Lane. Cross and continue (SE) with hedge R through Hammonds Farm into a track between brick gate posts out to Hammonds Lane.

5 Turn R (W) along the lane and in 400m at the signpost turn L through a gap. Follow the path (SW) with hedge R into a wood. On emerging from this continue (SW) with hedge L towards Sandridge, passing a small pond L. This path continues between fields across Langley Grove. Continue to the church L and into the High Street. Turn L back to the car park.

NOTE : Planting of trees by The Woodland Trust to create Heartwood Forest, started in 2010. It is planned that 600,000 trees will be planted on 350 hectares (over 850 acres) of land.

Sandridge Church

WALK 23

14th Century Stone Screen Chancel arch of Roman bricks, St Leonard's Church, Sandridge

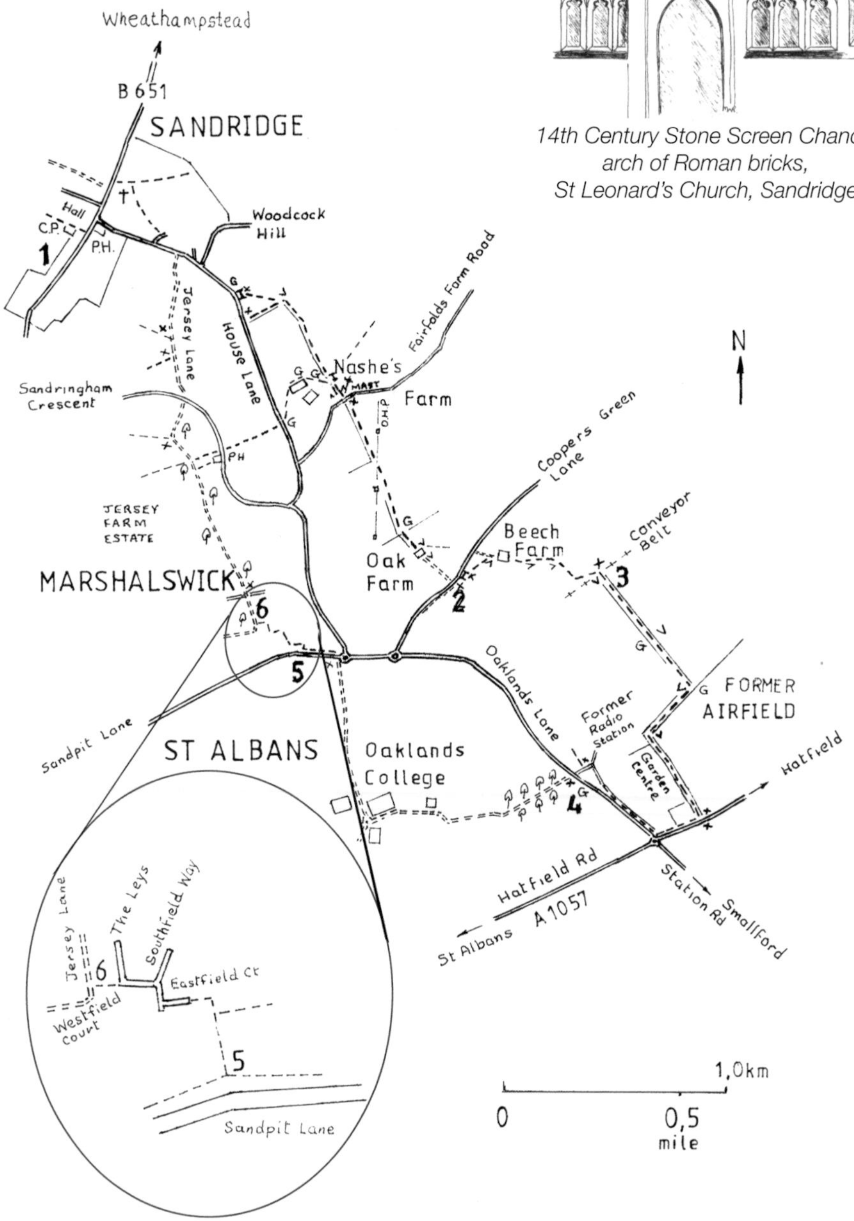

Total Distance 6.2 miles (10.0 km)

SANDRIDGE, OAKLANDS, JERSEY LANE

WALK 23

Park in Sandridge public car park by the village hall. G.R.169,104

1 From the car park, cross the B651 and turn L. In 100m turn R (SE) into House Lane. Keep on the asphalt path L by the housing and pass Woodcock Hill L. In a further 200m turn L at the signposted stile. This path goes diagonally uphill (E) to a waymarked hedge corner. Continue (SE) along a bridleway past Nashes Farm R, and cross Fairfolds Farm road. Continue (SE) with fence R to Oak Farm, then along the farm access road to Coopers Green Lane.

2 Turn L (NE) and in 60m turn R at the stile and signpost into a small wood. Continue (NE) onto an access road where turn R to Beech Farm. Follow the waymarks around the farm (E), then along a gravel road. This bends L then turns R (SE) at a small bridge over a conveyor belt.

3 A well-marked track continues (SE) between hedges, through a gate, then hedge R towards a large iron gate at the boundary of the former airfield. Here turn R (SW) in front of the gate, and with hedge L continue to a gap. Continue and turn L (SE) following the former airfield boundary L between chain link fences to meet the St Albans/Hatfield road (A1057). Turn R (SE) along the road passing Notcutts Garden Centre R. At the roundabout turn R (NW) into a service road alongside housing with hedge L, parallel with Oaklands Lane. This continues as a path into a road signed 'Radio Station', which turns L (W). Cross Oaklands Lane into the access road (W) to Oaklands College.

4 This tree-lined asphalt road continues (W) towards the main farm buildings. At the T-junction turn R (N) along a wide gravel track between farm buildings, which emerges onto Sandpit Lane. Cross and turn L (W) along the boundary of Jersey Farm housing estate.

5 After about 250m just before the path bends L, turn R (N) along a path by a house with a conservatory. Then turn L (W) into Eastfield Court. At the T-junction, turn R and in a few metres turn L (W) into Westfield Court. Where this bends R, continue ahead in front of housing into Jersey Lane.

6 Turn R (N) along this tree-lined lane and in about 2km this emerges onto House Lane. Here turn L (NW) along the lane to Sandridge village. Turn L (SW) along the B651 to the car park.

Alternatively : Turn R along tree-lined lane and in about 1.5km turn L into woodland park onto a bridleway (NW) to Highfield Road. Continue downhill to the St Albans Road, turn R to the car park L in about 250m.

This walk can be linked with No.22 to form a figure-of-eight all-day walk.

Oaklands

WALK 24

Well at Bovingdon

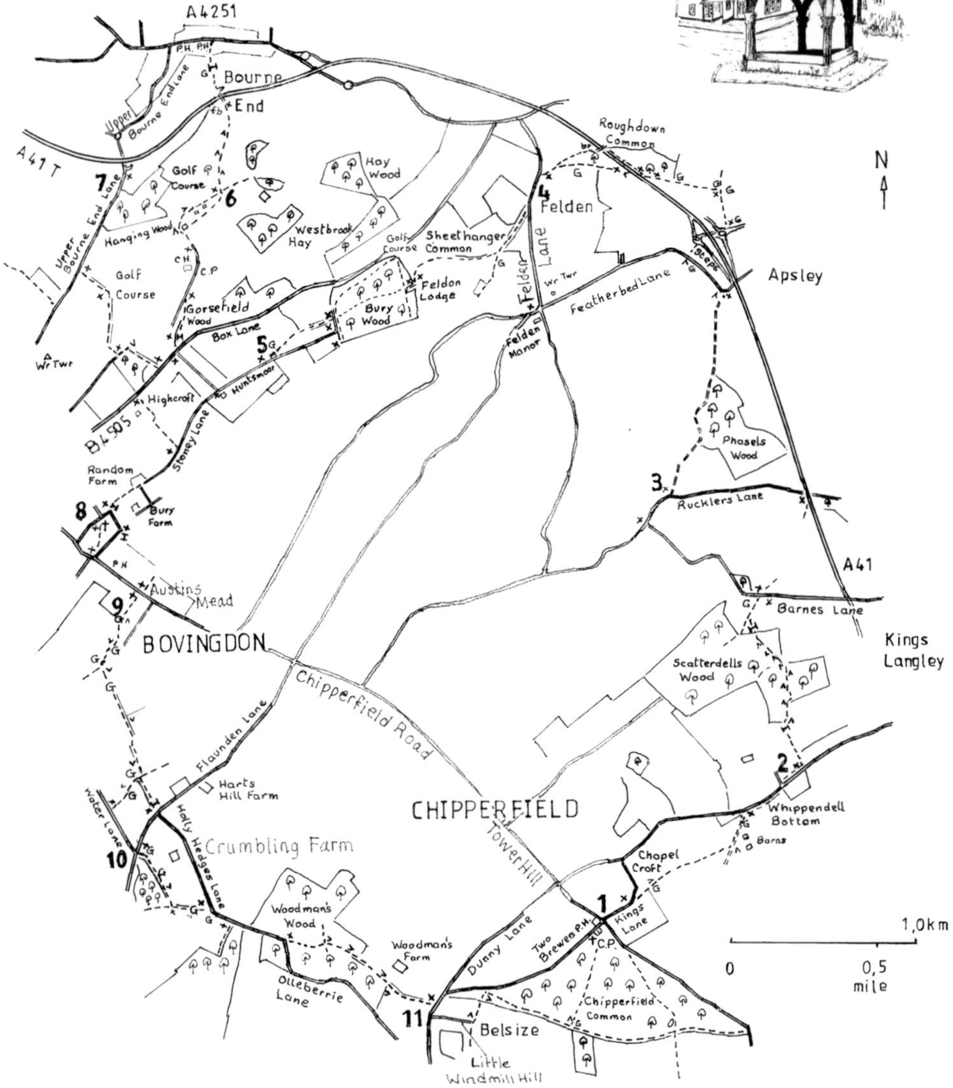

Total Distance 12.4 miles (20.0 km)
Shorter route 9.0 miles (14.5 km)

CHIPPERFIELD, FELDEN, BOURNE END, BOVINGDON

WALK 24

Park in Chipperfield public car park alongside St Paul's Church. G.R.044,016

1 Walk past the Two Brewers PH (NE) and cross the road into King's Lane. Where this road turns L, continue ahead (NE) along a gravel track, then cross an open field. In about 100m, bear L (N) across another field to a gate onto a road. Bear R (NE) along a path beside the road down to Whippendell Bottom. Cross road and take permissive path R uphill.

2 Turn L and continue along a fenced path into Scatterdells Wood. Cross the stile and turn R (E). In about 25m, turn L (N) and follow the tree waymarks (NW). Ignore a crossing track and continue ahead, following waymarks (NW) to a stile at the boundary of the wood. Cross into an open field (NE) to Barnes Lane. Turn L (W) along this lane for about 750m to its T-junction with Rucklers Lane. Turn R for 200m to a bridleway L.

3 Go along this bridleway (N) beside Phasels Wood, the Herts County Scout Camping Ground R. In about 1km on reaching Featherbed Lane, do not cross the Motorway bridge R, but turn L (NW) downhill along Featherbed Lane. In about 250m look for a gate R which leads to steps down to the nearest roundabout. Cross carefully under the A41 road bridge and at the next junction turn L through a gate onto a path (N) with hedge R. In 100m go through a gate, turn L through another gate (W) with hedge L. (This area is bright with chalk-loving flowers in spring and summer). Go through a metal field gate (W) along a wood boundary R. Cross the A41 bridge, bear L up steps onto a path and track through a wood (W), then through a gate to Felden Lane.

4 Turn L (S) up this lane and in 200m fork R (SW) along the drive to the gatehouse of Felden Lodge. Where a bridleway crosses, turn R (W) onto it and continue alongside the golf course. Where there is a wooden fence L keep alongside it and cross a wide bridleway. Continue (SW) by the Bury Wood Notice up steps to a residential road. Turn R for 20m, then L (W) on a path between house fences. Bear L across an open field to a signpost. Go through a gate into Stoney Lane and turn R.

5 Take the next turning R (NW) opposite 'Huntsmoor'. At Box Lane (B4505) turn R, cross the road with care and in 20m go L onto a tarmac driveway. Ignore the bridleway R, but take the footpath over a stile (N), through Gorsefield Wood to the golf club access road. Follow this road past the car park R, the clubhouse L and swing left past large buildings R. Ignore a footpath L, but continue past two bungalows R to a signpost.

6 Turn L (N) and follow the path downhill to the bridleway bridge over the A41. Cross to a zig-zag on this path, through a gate out to A4251 at Bourne End. Here turn L (W), where refreshments may be obtained at The White Horse PH or The Anchor PH.

7 Take Upper Bourne End Lane (SW), by the Complete Outdoors shop, past the industrial area R and go under the A41. Keep to this lane uphill, past Hanging Wood L until the lane levels. Turn L on a bridleway alongside the golf course L. Follow waymarks out to the main entrance in Box Lane (B4505). Cross, turn R (SW) and in 250m turn L onto a path just before Highcroft Farm entrance. Follow this through a R and L to Stoney Lane, where turn R (SW) to the outskirts of Bovingdon.

8 At the road, turn R then L into Bovingdon churchyard. Follow the tarmac path to the road, then R to the centre of the village. Note the well. Turn L (SE) past The Bull PH, cross the road and go up Chipperfield Road to the second turning to Austins Mead. At the fingerpost, turn R through housing and take the path between Nos.52 and 51.

continued over

continued from page 71

9 Go through a gate (SW) into a field with hedge R. Go through another gate (S) to the field corner opposite. At the gate bear L (SE) over a field to a gate at the end of the hedge L. Continue (SE) with hedge L, then cross an open field to a hedge R to a footpath junction. Turn R through a gate (SW) with hedge R. Go through another gate, then with wooden fence L meet Water Lane. Turn L (SE) down to Flaunden Lane.

10 Cross the lane and take the path (SE) with woodland R. Go through gate and continue to the R corner of the field. Go through the gap with pond R and immediately turn L (E) with hedge L. Go through a gate, then through another gate into Holly Hedges Lane, turn R (SE). Ignore the path R and bridleway L and where the road turns R, bear L (E) through the barrier into Woodmans Wood at the notice board. Follow the path downhill, cross a bridleway, then go uphill. On emerging from the wood continue ahead (E) with hedge L down to Dunny Lane in Belsize. Cross the lane and turn R (SW).

11 In 100m turn L up Little Windmill Hill. At the last bungalow turn L (N) along a path (NE). This joins another path, along which bear R (E). Continue through woodland with housing R for about 600m. Immediately before a gated barrier, turn L (NE) along a path signed 'Easy Access'. This emerges onto the cricket field on Chipperfield Common. Go behind the pavilion (N) by the church wall to the car park.

NOTE : This walk may be shortened at Item 5 by continuing along Stoney Lane (SW) to Bovingdon Church. Then continue from Item 8.

BIBLIOGRAPHY

LOCAL INFORMATION

1. 24 Footpath Walks Around St Albans, Bill Frost, St Albans & District Footpaths Society, 2009
2. Hertfordshire Rambles, Liz Moynihan, Countryside Books, 2000
3. Village Walks in Herts, Liz Moynihan, Countryside Books, 2003
4. Hertfordshire Chain Walk, East Herts Footpath Society, Castlemead, 1994
5. The Hertfordshire Way, Bert Richardson, Castlemead, 2005
6. Pub Strolls in Herts, Alan Charles, Countryside Books, 2002
7. Pub Walks in Herts, Alan Charles, Countryside Books, 2007
8. Pocket Pub Walks in Hertfordshire, Nick Corble, Countryside Books, 2007
9. 50 Walks in Hertfordshire, AA Publishing, 2009
10. Short Circular Walks on the New River & S.E. Herts, John N. Merrill, Walks & Write, 2005
11. Waterside Walks in Herts & Beds, Nick Corble, Countryside Books, 2008
12. Long Circular Walks in E. Herts, John N. Merrill, The John Merrill Foundation, 2007
13. Long Circular Walks in W. Herts, John N. Merrill, The John Merrill Foundation, 2007